Esbj!

The Heart and Mind of A Professor

Dennis J. Johnson
in collaboration with
Robert G. Esbjornson

This book is dedicated to all of the students
whose work, responses and relationships enabled
Robert G. Esbjornson to become "ESBJ!"

ISBN-10: 1-934478-09-1
ISBN-13: 978-1-934478-09-7

Acknowledgments

I wish to acknowledge the many persons who helped me with this manuscript. First and foremost, I thank the subject of the book, Esbj. Working with him and his writings was like having one long and satisfying conversation with him. This proved to be a personally enriching gift.

I also wish to thank my wife Carol who is always my first proofreader and writing compass. Thanks to Garrett Paul, professor in the present Gustavus religion department, and to retired Director of Public Affairs, Elaine Brostrom and her husband, retired mathematics professor, Milt Brostrom for reading the draft and making useful suggestions. Special thanks to Liz Sietsema, friend and former colleague, whose superb sense of style and word usage improved this manuscript. Thanks also to Jonathan Tillquist who has provided his computer and technical skills to keep me operational. Jonathan has a great appreciation for the creative efforts of writers and guards against manuscript loss through error or carelessness.

Finally, great thanks to Jim Peterson, president of Gustavus Adolphus College, for providing the funds to make this publication possible.

A note: The use of inclusive language came into vogue in the middle of Esbj's career. I asked him if he wanted to make editorial changes to update the language. Esbj, a great supporter of women's issues and language change, sensed that documents are historical and, as such, ought to remain true to the time in which they were written.

Proceeds from the sale of this book will benefit the Robert G. Esbjornson Fund within the Christ Chapel Endowment.

Table of Contents

Per Esbjornson congratulates his son on graduation day, 1941.

Esbj!

Introduction

Es-bjorn-son, literally "son of a bear god." The name is too long to resist shortening. So, the subject of this book became known as Esbj. Esbj is pronounced Es-be, and sometimes spelled the same, other times Esby. However one spells it, it seems most appropriate to use it with an exclamation point. Esbj!

During his career, Robert Esbjornson was one of the most honored faculty members in the Gustavus community. He received the Edgar M. Carlson Award for Innovative Teaching (the College's most prestigious faculty award), he was nominated twice for a National Teacher of the Year Award, and he received the Gustavus Adolphus College Association of Congregation's Covenant Award for contributions relating Church to College. But the most moving accolades come from former students. Their testimonies document the influence of a professor upon a life and should give encouragement to every person who steps into a classroom thinking that he or she can make a difference. The student comments also provide clues as to what it takes to make that difference.

Esbjornson's career is also worthy of study as a model for what it means to be a professor at a college of the Church. For anyone who doubts that faith and reason can be held together or that academic integrity can exist side by side with a faith commitment, Esbjornson's writings on the topic are illuminating.

I have had the privilege of knowing Robert Esbjornson for nearly a half century. During that time Esbj has been, at various times, my landlord, my teacher, my parishioner, my colleague and always, first and foremost, my friend and conversation partner. Knowing Esbj has been a trip! I not only knew him in his professional role, but I knew him as a family man, husband, father, and grandfather. I have known him as a younger man and in his older age. I have come to know something of his heart and mind.

Therefore, when Esbj asked that I assist him in organizing his papers, letters, sermons and other writings, I could only respond enthusiastically. We agreed that this work was not to be a biography as such, although biographical material is included so that the reader has a more complete understanding of the person. Thus, this is Esbj's "memoir," and the narrative is primarily in his words. This also contains my words about Esbj with some references to the context in which he did his work. I have chosen to use his and my initials, RE and DJ, to assist the reader in keeping our voices distinct. In gathering this collection of his thoughts, I have researched sermons, chapel talks, newsletter writings, essays and his major papers. I have also relied on conversations with Esbj. I have necessarily edited and excerpted from those sources to make the wealth of material accessible to the general reader.

In reviewing Esbj's writings one marvels at the wide range of interests that engaged him. His restless mind kept him probing into many fields. His was the true liberal arts approach that called for dialogue and conversation among the many disciplines of the academy. In one sense, Esbj was a renaissance man standing in the midst of specialists. Esbj did not have the PhD. His highest degrees were the Master of Divinity (M.Div) from Augustana Seminary and the Master of Sacred Theology (STM) from Yale Divinity School. Not having the terminal degree caused some colleagues to dismiss him as "not a serious scholar." Today, Gustavus would not likely hire such a person to be a member of its faculty. That is understandable. Yet, in a time of ever increasing specialty and isolation of department to department, the need for an Esbj remains more important than ever. His personality and aptitude caused him to constantly inquire about the relevance and implications of the research findings of one discipline for another. His task was to crossover and offer that discipline views from his field of inquiry. And, he was quick to take back with him information and views that would cause him to rethink his own positions. His mission was to connect the dots.

He was particularly interested in the ancient question first posed by Tertullian in the second century after Christ's death, "What has Jerusalem to do with Athens?" Athens represents the intellectual center and secular spirit of society. Jerusalem represents the religious mind and the spiritual quest. Esbj understood historically that Athens and Jerusalem were in tension, but not in conflict, and he was committed to the continued conversation between the two.

He wrote prolifically on the nature of Gustavus as a Church-related College. He kept in balance his academic concerns and his passionate commitment to "God and the highest search for Truth." Esbj stood between those who taught as unquestioning defenders of the faith and those who believed that one should only teach as a disinterested observer. He was the man in the middle or, better yet, he was Gustavus' bridge between the past and future, the bridge between departments and the bridge within his own department where divergent personalities and viewpoints created tension and division. He believed strongly in the value of the community and the need for diversity and the need for faithfulness to tradition. He could hold the strains and tensions of such a stance in a creative way.

In the end, Esbj worried that his own experience of the relationship of College and Church was fading away. He was a worrier about College issues long after he retired. He anguished because he was a lover. He was a lover of the Church and a lover of the Academy and especially a lover of Gustavus and its students. To borrow from Frost, he had a "lover's quarrel" with both the Church and the College and he deplored any signs of a drift of College from Church and Church from College.

Today, there are those at the College who carry the same concerns and passions. Some of those have been influenced by Esbj while others knew him not. Yet, they are his successors, the keepers of the flame.

The words of Gustavus Business and Economics Professor Kyle Montague in the citation for the *Edgar M. Carlson Award for Innovative Teaching* and the testimonies of students which follow tell us of the esteem in which Esbj was held by students and colleagues. Their words will introduce you, as much as anything could, to Esbj and may make you curious to know more about the man who can inspire such comments. It has been said that "nobody cares about what you know, until they know you care." In that sense the medium is the message. This is a man who cared deeply about his students and his subject matter and, thereby, opened their hearts and minds to learning. It is my hope that the following pages will open to you the heart and mind of Esbj.

Dennis Johnson
September, 2007

Man of the Hour

"The Professor of the Year Award is certainly not something that Professor Esbjornson needs. The award that would be best tailored for this man would be the "Man of the Hour" award. Each hour that I spent with Esbj was a challenging, profitable, and rewarding one." **J. Randolf Beahrs '71**

The Edgar M. Carlson Award for Innovative Teaching
Robert Esbjornson
Religion – 1979

The Edgar M. Carlson Award for Innovative Teaching was established by the Board of Trustees of Gustavus Adolphus College to honor Dr. Edgar M. Carlson for his years of distinguished leadership as president and in recognition of his commitment to academic excellence. Each year, as a result of a nomination process involving faculty, students, and administrators, the award, in the amount of $1,500 is presented to a member of the Gustavus faculty in recognition of effective and innovative teaching. The recipient of this year's award is Professor Robert Esbjornson of the Department of Religion.

Professor Esbjornson has been a member of the faculty since 1950, and has been a creative and innovative teacher during his entire tenure as a member of the Department of Religion. His courses, though solid in conformity with their catalog descriptions, never remain static. Lecture notes that have yellowed with age may be found in his files but never in his briefcase. There is always a fresh approach, a relevant application, a timely treatment. His special interest is ethics and ranges from particular attention to the professions and vocations to the wider concerns of the environment. Though he regards his classroom as his primary arena, his concerns extend to students wherever they are and for years after they have left this place.

One of his colleagues describes Bob in the following words, "....no other person--teacher, administrator, student or staff--has so consistently urged renewal, rethinking, reform, all in the spirit of rejoicing. He brings to his colleagues and....to his classes an air of excitement." Another of his co-workers says, "Everything I have heard about Robert Esbjornson's classroom instruction leads me to conclude that he is challenging, thoughtful, dynamic, sympathetic, and, above all, imaginative in his approach to his students and his subject matter. These are the qualities that make an innovative teacher."

One does not speak of you, Bob, as a person, without including your lovely wife, Ruth. Together, in a very special and important way, you represent what this college tries to say and what it tries to be. A good friend of yours, in words better than mine, says this about both of you. "They bring a sense of concern for everyone and everything. If they ever knew how to be hostile, they have forgotten how to use that knowledge. It isn't that they can't and don't make hard decisions--they can and do--but they always 'speak the truth in love.'"

Bob, I think you know what I mean when I say that I am so pleased to be the one who, on behalf of your students and your colleagues, is privileged to present you with the Edgar M. Carlson Award for 1979.

Presented by Kyle Montague, Professor of Economics and Business, 1978 Recipient of the Carlson Award

Praise for a beloved professor

The following are more than paeans of praise. They give deep insight into what makes education meaningful and what makes a great teacher. These excerpts are from letters written in 1983 on the occasion of Esbj's retirement as a full-time professor. They were written by students who today are pastors, teachers, social workers, doctors, lawyers, businesspersons, artists and homemakers. They are representative of the many tributes that Esbj received over the years.

"How can I express my gratitude toward you that would really show how I feel? You are the one teacher that helped me get through life at Gustavus. I have such fond memories of that class (Studies in Religion 101) with the videotapes and final projects. Then there was Ethics and Medicine which taught me more about life than I could ever tell you. I have often thought back on that class and used what I learned in life situations. Then there was YOU. You alone had the greatest impact on me. I still, to this day, can't walk past Christ Chapel or think about a beautiful fall day with leaves falling and not think of you enjoying it too. You always had such a beautiful outlook on life and knew what the world had to offer that was both good and bad. With you I learned about life and I learned about love and how to treat each. I learned of compassion for people and the importance of just stopping and thinking about a nice summer day. I grew at Gustavus, and you, Esbj, were the water, soil and sunshine that made me grow."
Dave Najarian '81

"Like some shot of bolt lightning, boundary-crossing
 you led us
as dazed and dazzled eighteen-year-old pilgrims
 into new horizons.
Connecting, always searching the frontier,
 Your workplace was the college classroom
a cluttered office and noontime cafeteria table,
 You prodded, teased,
and sometimes played the fool
 to forge the fragile link of heart and head.

Deep down in us you felt our restless hunger
 and touched your own.
You dared believe we were Sons and Daughters
 of some grand Mysterious Quest!
Helped us listen, test the voices, ride the winds
 of far-flung destiny.

Guided by philosophers, poet and ancient manuscripts,
 we walked with you into monasteries,
down littered city streets.
 Your life for us seemed beckoned
by some yonder star.
 We moved together toward another New Bethlehem.
The Holy One sings with us this spring, Good Warrior!
 The Creator knows the seeds you once sowed have
burst into life.
 And still others, quiet, sure and full of promise,
 await,
 yet to bloom."   **Jon Magnuson '67**
                              Written on Easter Day, 1983

"To A Dancing Prof. I remember you as a provoker of thought, as a kind man who knew his students as people, as a fellow reader of "Report to Greco," but most of all as a Dancing Prof, speaker of good cheer and merry curiosity, someone with a hopeful, eager view of life, who raced forward into life headlong because wonderful things were ahead." **Andrea Pearson, '78**

"...yet beyond those remembrances of friend and mentor is the vision of a man whose concern for Planet Earth, whose caring for students through the academic and personal growth of college's years, whose creative sharing through teaching, and whose presence in pew and pulpit all witness to your love and faith in Creator God." **Lynn Freund Pettit '71**

"It is hard to imagine a Gustavus without you in the classroom, dancing ungodly jigs Godly to illustrate what might otherwise have been dull theological concepts. It's hard to imagine future Gusties missing out on guessing games of 'I wonder what Esbj's going to pull off at the 'Happening' today?' or 'What the devil does he mean by all this 'X' stuff?' You made things happen inside of us. You guided us to scrutinize, to turn the subject around and around, to pick at it. But not only that, and this is what separated you from many other teachers, and I love you for it--you guided us back to prisms through which we could renew our look at Life and see its wonder. You showed us the Joy of Searching, and since then that's what we've all been doing." **Tim Olson '77**

"I will always remember you as a professor who always seemed to have time for anyone who needed a little or a lot of it. This was not an uncommon trait among professors at Gustavus in the '60s, but you were exceptionally adept at giving not only your time and your heart to your students, but also a subtle something extra, a special ability to sympathize with our inexperience in life without calling it that, while at the same time graciously communicating the fruits of your own greater experience and deeper faith without ever seeming to be any more or less than our friend. It seemed to me that all students were equal in your eyes. All of us were worthy of your fatherly friendship and encouragement. Of course, you spotted and encouraged promising academics, but never at the expense of less gifted students." **Eric Stenman '67**

"Far beyond the classroom, your compassion, coupled with intellectual toughness convinces me that a Christian life is possible in this age--and I need reminding again and again. Thank you for letting in the light. The detailed journal we kept in the beginning of Christian Ethics was the first time I had formally written my thoughts for anyone other than myself. It was a time of realization that I might have ideas to share this way with others. Thank you for that seed of encouragement and ambition. Your startling imagination and playful approach to teaching are refreshing. My whimsy is nourished by your whimsy. Remembering your bright red socks makes me smile. A conversation with you makes me laugh. Thanks for the fun!" **Sue Busch Leaf '75**

A Poem

"I was afraid
of the turbulence
churning
inside me....

You showed me
the life and delight
in exploring the depths of yourself....
encountering both the demons and the angels
of Self;

and by example
encouraged me to unearth again and again
my own Self,
and therefore to live
a truly genuine life!"

Nancy L. Brown '79

"I recall three very important ways in which you affected my life. One was my honors thesis, that incredibly complex and overly ambitious project which began as an attempt to blame the environmental crisis on orthodox Christianity. Your concern for the Earth and your willingness to think in large perspectives with me led me to choose you as my adviser. I will always be grateful for the patience and insight and guidance you gave me as we shared thoughts and experiences. There is another time you and I shared which is more important to me now, looking back, than I thought it was at the time. When I was in your "Urban Church" group during winter term, you and everyone in the class had to know that I was challenging and rejecting the religious beliefs I'd grown up with. You, in your wisdom, did not argue with me or threaten me or make me feel guilty--you simply shared yourself. Although it was ten years before I returned to a church home, the time was not spent in anger, cynicism or bitterness, but in open exploration for what was meaningful. Your attitude at that crucial point had an impact on how I spent that time. Now that I have found my home again, I've abandoned my struggle to work out perfect beliefs and live instead in faith and grace. And now I can appreciate more fully the faith and love you showed at the time." **Diane L. Dornburg '73**

"I'm sending you something that I wrote on one of my 'Esbj days'--a day that I felt like I too had a bush of floppy hair to push back, glasses falling off my nose, and a crooked wonderful smile. I remember it as a day that I lived every second of every minute and thought of you often. The beauty of that day was that it began after a Religion class at GAC, when a beloved gray-haired friend infected me with his love of God's world and sent me out to really live it to my fullest:

Children's Dance

I could not come to school because
I'm in love with the world today.
I would not find it possible to
    stick with books and words,
        pencils and shelves,
        bells and noise.
I should not come to infect you
    with my madness;
for if I did, you too would run--
    and throw leaves up in the breeze
        to the sun
    and dig your fingers in moss
        beneath the pines
    and roll in fields
    and watch the clouds
    and crunch an apple with juice
        on your chin
    and never have to go in.
I may not come to school tomorrow

Barbara Jean Moore Stransky '72

"A highly charged spirit he is, a thoughtful man always on his way to the next event. Curious enough to question how and why we live. Filled with an understanding spirit that allows room for others in which to live, to love, to grow, to make mistakes and to be forgiven. Sparkling eyes that communicate humor, sometimes merriment and an intense interest in being a functioning part of the here and now. Serious eyes that show a sense of concern and caring that become a trademark for him. Evident above all else was a deep commitment to his God and a sense of humility that allowed him to walk in the state of grace whether he thought he deserved it or not. He helped me believe in myself, in a positive outlook on life and in an understanding Creator." **Jane Falconer**

Confirmation, circa 1933.

Chapter One

Finding a Vocation

DJ: Esbj has a great fascination with story, the human story, his personal story, the stories that others tell. Throughout his teaching and preaching, Esbj sought to connect those stories with God's Story. The Bible Story provides clues, insights, and directions for one's personal story and creates a framework for understanding one's life in relation to God's work in the world. So, we naturally begin with Esbj's personal story.

Robert Esbjornson is the eldest of two boys born in Duluth, Minnesota in 1918. His mother died when he was but eight years old. He was old enough to remember, too young to fully understand. Esbj remembers kneeling with his father at his mother's bedside praying the Lord's Prayer. His mother died that evening. Esbj writes of this experience and the influence on him:

RE: After Mother died, my dad chose to take care of us, but he had to work. So he found families who would take us into their homes. In a sense we were foster children. That went on for five years, and then, alas, I got tuberculosis of the stomach. It was too much for these families and my father, so my relatives took care of me for a year while I recovered. There I discovered a wider community, the extended family of Solomon and Ida Swenson, my mother's family. There were four aunts and one uncle and their mates and several cousins. Because of their care, I learned to live as a trusting person, learning to live with others and for others.

Then, at the age of 15, my father remarried and we children got a step-mother. Anna, at the age of 33, took on the task of getting two teen-age boys, one in poor health and neither with work experience, into shape. Dad worked as a skilled craftsman in Duluth. Anna ran the farm she had inherited from her parents while we boys helped. We prospered enough to make it possible for John and me to get a college education and for them to live a reasonably comfortable life.

DJ: Esbj has always found guidance in life by listening to his own story and by listening to God. He believed that guidance came through people and at times one would least expect it. He tells the following story:

RE: One day in my confirmation class, Pastor Carl Olson gave some advice: Pray, he said, for guidance in choosing your life work, your life partner, and read the Bible. I took his advice seriously. I was 15 and beginning to wonder what I would do with my life. One day in a senior social studies class the conversation turned to careers. I said, I know what I don't want to be and that is a teacher or a preacher! I was going to be a journalist, a foreign correspondent and I went to Duluth Junior College with that in mind. I had my plan.

Apparently God had another idea in mind, and his guidance came through an angel, my English teacher. She gave me the grade of unsatisfactory for every theme I wrote. Okay, not a journalist, so then what? Guidance, God, if you please. I took the Strong Vocational Interest Test, twice, because I didn't believe the results the first time. I should consider working with people, teaching or the ministry. Gulp! So I planned to teach. I would teach speech and drama, for I had some interest and talent in acting and speaking.

I was a counselor at a Bible camp the summer after my sophomore year. I head a sermon about the need for teachers in Africa. Aha! My heart responded. Guidance came through a preacher at a vesper service by the side of a lake.

I came to Gustavus in the fall of 1939 with a plan to prepare for being a missionary teacher in Africa. I was in a high school methods class in my junior year. I was bored. I fell asleep. The professor suggested that I either pay attention or leave. I left. We had three teachers of philosophy and religion who were very stimulating. One of them was Edgar Carlson. I found new interest in a class in ethics. I wrote an essay about ethics that won a prize. Guidance through someone's decision to give me a prize? I think so.

I decided to go to the seminary with a commitment to go to Africa to teach. A recruiter for the Board of World Missions came to the campus. I interviewed and declared myself to be a candidate. Yet, I had a vague discontent as if I had done something dishonest. Guidance from deep within my heart? I think so.

I suppressed that feeling throughout my years at the seminary. I carried on with my plan. I was accepted to be a missionary. After seminary, I would go to the Kennedy School of Missions in Hartford, Connecticut. Then, in the spring term of my third year, the program crashed. The feeling of uncertainty that I had suppressed came to the surface. I went through anguish. What now should I do? The seminary faculty had an alternative plan. I could go to a town called Newington, a suburb of Hartford and do survey work for the Board of American Missions, to see whether there were people who would like to have a new Lutheran Church. The summer would give me time to think.

DJ: At the same time, Bob was engaged to be married to Ruth. Ruth's parents had deep reservations about their daughter going off to Africa and Ruth had similar reservations as well. She wrote to Bob to express her doubts. Again, for Bob, this was guidance.

RE: Instead, I chose to continue the work that I had started in Newington and I was called to be the first pastor. I would be a missionary in America, not Africa, but in a suburb in New England, a place I would never have dreamed of working. During the next five years I did graduate studies in social ethics at Yale Divinity School. On October 31, 1949, Dr George Hall, one of my Gustavus religion teachers, came to preach at a Reformation service in Hartford. Ruth and I went to hear him and after the service we went to talk with him. I introduced him to the mother of a Gustavus student and he said to her, 'We may be taking your pastor away from you soon.' What a surprise! I knew at once that this was the place for me. At once! I had been right all along about what to do, teaching, but wrong about where to do it. Gustavus seemed the best place on earth for me, and I believe it has been.

DJ: Esbj taught through story, often using his own story to illustrate the point. By describing the twists and turns and lack of foreknowledge, Esbj made the following point for the students listening to one of his chapel talks:

RE: You are an actor in a story, but not its author. You live in a drama, and you are never sure what is going to happen next. It is an exciting way to see your life, because you know your actions have consequences, and that there are surprises ahead that you did not expect and could not plan for. Your life may turn out to be quite different from what you are planning to be. There will be losses, defeats, sad experiences as well as victories and successes. They are all part of the story. You don't see its end, maybe not even its purpose. The wisdom that you need is about being who you are wherever you are, and trusting God to guide you all your days, humbly accepting life as it comes and responding to it with love, courage and creativity.

DJ: Esbj found his true calling and trusted that students would find theirs.

This chapel talk, given in May of 1980, deals with significance, insignificance, randomness and purposefulness. Esbj titled it, "The Divine You."

RE: Intelligence, informed by extrapolations from observed events, tells me that I was started as a random event, probably one night in August 63 years ago. If at the moment of my existence a minute particle, a sperm, had wriggled off course on its way to another tiny particle, an ovum, if it had veered ever so slightly in any of infinitely many possible ways, then I never would have existed at all. Another would have existed in my place perhaps, but it would not have been me. I am a unique, random event that just happened.

Intelligence tells me that what is true about my beginning is true also of my father's and my mother's beginnings and so on back to our remotest ancestors. And it is true of your beginning as well. At each moment of conception a one in a million event occurs and 999,999,999 did not. Intelligence tells me what an infinitely small chance happening I am!

And it adds, in a short while you will cease to exist. Your end is inevitable. You have no control strong enough to prevent it. You will die, and in the infinite series of events in a vast cosmos, happenings will continue as if you had never existed. Someday, in the future, your heart will beat one last time. Your lungs will expel their last breath. Your tastes, loves, regrets, successes and failures will vanish. The rest of the universe will go on until it too shall end. Intelligence tells me, you are a chance event in an infinite series. You flash briefly on that infinite screen and then you go dark.

How is it then, Mr. Intelligence, that I do not feel insignificant? Why do I feel my birth as a momentous event? Why is my life experience aglow with a vivid sense of value? Why do I not accept your dispassionate judgment based on sensible observation?

On July 4, 1939 another random event happened in a farm house in Carlton County, Minnesota. I happened to be in the house when a car happened to come up the driveway. Out of the car stepped a man, he also one of those random events that happened by chance to be conceived when one tiny particle kept on course--and so forth. He happened by when I happened to be at home on a holiday when I might have been away and he might have gone to a beach party. He was a student recruiter, and he persuaded me to come to Gustavus in spite of my worries about finances. "Money is no problem," he happened to say. You would agree, I am sure, that it was so then when tuition was $75 a semester. So it happened that I came to Gustavus. Intelligence tells me that it was one chance in a thousand that he and I should meet that day--another random event. If he had not come I would very likely not be here speaking in this place today.

Why, Mr. Intelligence, do I not see it that way? Why do I value that event, that chance happening in an infinite number of random movements in the universe? There was a woman who happened to be assigned a chapel seat that happened to be in the row just in front of me. She happened to be at Gustavus because of a series of happenings that began years before when a tiny particle,..... and so forth.

I liked her. I suppose, Mr. Intelligence, that you want to inform me that I happened to like her, sort of randomly. One day the librarian (who just happened to be a librarian because her husband happened to die too soon) said to me, "Boo (Ruth's nickname based on her family name of Bostrom) would make a fine partner for you." And, I say to you, Mr. Intelligence, how is it that to this day, I value, I rejoice in her remark? Boo and I were married. I ask you, Mr. Intelligence, why is it that such an infinitely small happening among the millions and trillions of random events is so valuable to me that I celebrate it today?

I can think of two answers. Either it is valuable, important and significant because *I say it is,* because I am the center of value, because I assign value to my birth, my life, my marriage. Or I experience these affairs as delights because they are given to me as gifts from a wildly generous, astonishingly gracious God. I choose one or the other answer. I choose between regarding myself as the center and creator of my own value, or God as one who commands and whose commands establish my life. Since I know, as an intelligent being, that I am interrelated to much more than myself and am so interdependent in a network of sustaining relationships, I choose to honor God as the giver of life. And I often stop to wonder that there is something rather than nothing; galaxies and molecules and quirky people and quarks, an infinite love creating each of us, even as we make our lives out of the gifts we have received.

It may be absurd. Or it may be too good to be merely true. If it is the latter, no wonder we have a catalyst for celebration with every birth, every marriage, and other events beyond mention and even, through tears of grief, with the end of lives unique and wonderful that we value even after they have gone.

Gustavus Graduation, 1941

Chapter Two

The Making of a Social Ethicist

DJ: Entering Gustavus in 1939, Esbj took a course from Professor Edgar M. Carlson in Christian social ethics which had a profound influence on the young scholar and tapped into his natural compassion, sense of justice and fair play. Esbj came to Gustavus intending to major in history and to become a teacher. Carlson pointed him to the major issues facing the world and society and convinced him that theology and the Church had much to say and much to offer the hurting world. Bob was utterly fascinated by thinking about humans as moral agents. The war debate was in full swing during his student days. Edgar Carlson and George Hall, both from the Christianity Department, were pacifists. Dr.Conrad Peterson (history) and Oscar Winfield (philosophy) were defenders of the "just war" theory. Debates were everywhere. What should students do about the draft? Draft status applications made no provision for a student to register as a conscientious objector. Students were advised to "write it in." Esbj was one student who did just that. However, it was the debate atmosphere about ethics that stimulated Esbj to pursue social ethics as a field of study.

Following Gustavus, Esbj went to Augustana Seminary in Rock Island, Illinois. Almost all Gustie pre-seminarians went to Rock Island to prepare for ministry. Young men from Republican familes came to the seminary, it was observed, but very few graduated with that political philosophy intact. That was due to the impact of A.D. Mattson who taught the Old Testament prophets and Christian Ethics. Mattson had a profound influence through his physical presence (he looked like a prophet), passion and frankness. Augustana Seminary was called "The School of the Prophets" and Mattson embodied that spirit. He was especially fond of the prophet Amos and Esbj thought A.D. (as he was affectionately called) was the very personification of Amos. A.D. told his classes that he loved the "old time religion--as long as it was as old as Moses, Amos and Jesus." He thundered against poverty, political corruption and the exploitation of the poor. He referred to *laissez- faire* theories of the marketplace as the "lazy fairy." He told homespun stories to drive his point home. He was a follower of Walter Rauschenbusch who worked in Hell's Kitchen in Brooklyn where he developed the "Social Gospel." If Christians were called to pick up the beaten man left on the road between Jerusalem and Jericho, Rauschenbusch asked, at what point should the Christian think about making the road free of thieves and safe for travel? Why not address the systemic issues and not just be there to apply the bandages? Rauschenbusch believed that if we implemented the ethics of Jesus we could build the Kingdom of God on earth. As a Lutheran, Mattson rejected that notion of perfectibility. He knew the problem was not just the unjust systems of economics, but the stubbornness of sin. Nevertheless, A.D was just as vigorous in calling for action. A well known hymn was often sung at chapel, "Rise up O Men of God, His kingdom tarries long; bring in the day of brotherhood, and end the night of wrong." The hymn had its Lutheran critics, as if the Kingdom's arrival depended on our efforts, yet A.D. asked if the Lutheran way was to substitute the words, "Sit down O men of God, there is nothing you can do."

Writing in 1938, Mattson addressed questions of church and state, the church and politics. These are thoughts that shaped Esbj and are still relevant in 2007 and helpful to the debate about religion and politics.

The church is not a political unit, and therefore we could not mix church and state even if we tried to do so. This does not imply that the church has nothing to do with the affairs of the state. The Christian is not only a Christian, but also a citizen, and when the Christian functions as a citizen he can not leave his religion out of the picture. Christians should be guided by their Christian convictions when they go to the polls, when they serve in legislative halls, or whenever they function in a civic capacity. It is the duty of the church to enlighten the conscience of its membership to the end that the will of God may be done in the affairs of men. We cannot have the church in politics, but we can and must have religion in politics if our social order is to survive.

It would be a mistake for the church to identify itself with any political group or faction…The church must hold aloof from all partisan politics in order that she may judge all things from the point of view of Christian principles. This does not mean that she has nothing to do with the character of politics but rather the contrary. She must denounce sin wherever sin is found, and she must take a positive stand for righteousness and justice. Thus the church will bring its influence to bear upon the state and its affairs.

No one can read the great prophets of the Old Testament without becoming aware of their tremendous passion for social righteousness. A.D. Mattson, *Christian Ethics*, 1947 pp.346-350

A.D. was active in the labor unions and much honored by them as one of the few clergy who worked on behalf of the rights of laborers.

Esbj was at the seminary (1941-1945) at a time when war was going on around the world. Thinkers were looking at what kind of a world would be built after the war. How would our society deal with enemies, refugees, how would

America rebuild and how could the nation forge an enduring peace? Esbj pondered how he could make a contribution. He had been preparing for service on Augustana's mission fields, but he was now entering into service as a parish pastor. One door was closing and another was being opened, although the shape of what was beyond that door was anything but clear to him. Yet, in hindsight, Esbj could see the hand of God at work in his life.

Ordination, 1945.

Esbj and Ruth began their ministry in Newington. The task was to develop a new congregation. One of the attractions in the call for Esbj was that Newington was not far from Yale and Esbj had permission to do part-time graduate work at the Divinity School.

Building on his natural bent for ethical studies which had been challenged and nurtured by Carlson at Gustavus and Mattson at Augustana, Esbj concentrated his graduate studies in social ethics.

RE: My interest in ethics became an intense personal concern at the time when the appalling evils of the Nazi tyranny became known. An article appeared in *The Christian Century*, titled "From Luther to Hitler," that made the case for blaming Luther and Lutheran teaching about politics and government that led down a slippery slope to the hell of Dachau. I had more than an academic concern in my studies of Lutheran social ethics. I was moved by the need to know whether Lutheranism was a major antecedent of Nazism, for I did not think I could remain in the Lutheran household if it was so.

DJ: It was to be characteristic of Esbj's work that his very soul was involved in his academic pursuits. Reflecting his mood during that time, Esbj later wrote, "It was not just intellectual curiosity that motivated me, it was fire in my heart. It was a deep sense of outrage and dread." Does anyone do his or her studies in an entirely objective fashion? I do not believe so, certainly Esbj as a believer sought, as we often do, for the position that might re-enforce belief. Yet, he was cognizant of that very danger and was on guard against it. In looking back on that time, Esbj described his soul's unrest about the ethics questions raised by the Holocaust. Esbj kept digging.

RE: Do you know what I found out? There was another story. It took digging, research, academic style, to find it. But it was there. It was in the stories of people like Bishop Berggrav and his colleagues in the Norwegian Church, and of Kai Munk in Denmark, a dramatist and rural pastor, the witness of the Dutch Church, and the stories of Dietrich Bonhoeffer and the Confessing Church and Hans Lilje in Germany, and the student Christian resistance movement in France. Not only did their stories of resistance help me but their reasons for resisting were firmly grounded in the Bible and in the historic confessions of the Church.

DJ: Esbj was also greatly moved by the story of the pastor who rescued hundreds of boys and girls living at Bethel, a Lutheran institution for the mentally and physically handicapped. Such children were marked for extermination by the Nazis. The story is told in Edna Hong's *Bright Valley of Love*.

The discovery of such stories reaffirmed Esbj's faith and his vocational choice of being a teacher at a college of the church. This was at the heart of Esbj's passionate defense of the uniqueness of the Christian liberal arts college. His investigations from Nazi Germany revealed the failure of education, science, medicine in the face of evil. His core conviction convinced him that education needed "something more" and that "something more" was love.

RE: I believe that love for one another needs instruction in the arts of loving, inspiration in the stories of love, strength drawn from the ground of love, who is God.

DJ: The Gustavus into which Esbj came as a professor was one that saw its mission in a postwar world very clearly. Students were exposed to the ideals of Christian education articulated by Esbj's former Gustavus teacher and now president of the College, Edgar M. Carlson, and a group of professors who had lived through the Great War. The task that they saw was that of rebuilding the world along saner lines than had been experienced in the first half of the 20th century. They were idealists who knew that college education was about preparing men and women to lead in the last half of the century. They believed it would take men and women of courage, character and commitment who would employ their best thinking on behalf of the well being of society. They wanted young people to know "the mind of Christ" and that faithful living required an allegiance to the Christ of faith.

His particular interest in ethics got another boost while in graduate school at Yale, again from a *Christian Century* article:

RE: My interest in Christianity and politics, and the relations of church and state, made me respond to another article in *The Christian Century* about a Lutheran governor in Minnesota who claimed to connect his religious beliefs with his politics. It was an article about Luther Youngdahl's campaign against slot machines that succeeded in making them illegal. My studies made me skeptical about such claims, so I began my investigation in a mood of suspicion. Scholars now call this "the hermeneutics of suspicion."

DJ: A thorough investigation of Youngdahl's rhetoric, programs, tactics and philosophy led Esbj to conclude that Youngdahl did indeed try to do what he claimed. Esbj's work resulted in his thesis for his master's degree (STM) at

Yale. The work was later published as a book, *A Christian in Politics: Luther W. Youngdahl, 1955*

In the introduction to the book, Esbj outlined his "concluding affirmations about God and politics":

1. Political authority is an inescapable fact of life, because God has created man as a member of society. It consists of coercion and respect, assertion of and submission to authority.

2. Politics operates under the law of mutual helpfulness which God has ordained. In order to obtain and hold the respect of those who submit to their authority, men in power must provide for the security and general welfare of the people; and the people must in turn obey the laws and the upholders of the law. The Christian politician accepts government as the instrument whereby God enforces his law of mutual help in human society. He therefore participates willingly if not always lightheartedly, in the political process of conflict and compromise.

3. Because of human sinfulness, politics can become corrupt. Authority can be abused by leaders. Law can benefit the few at the expense of the many or ignore the interests of those who have no influence. Special interests can usurp the dominating roles in the political process. No individual or group is unambiguously good or evil. Even a Christian politician and a Christian group can be subject to the corrosive effects of self-interest and power lust.

4. Because politics can become demonic, the Christian citizen acknowledges that the whole political process of conflict and compromise is an essential check on the self-will and the power lust of special interest groups and individuals. He humbly accepts his role within the process and admits the necessity of having opponents and critics as a curb on himself and his party.

5. The Christian citizen is aware of the need for political wisdom. He knows that he must be a political scientist in the broadest sense of the word. He must accurately take stock of the situation in which he is involved and adopt an effective strategy for achieving his goals. He knows that piety is no substitute for political shrewdness. To be effective, he must know the facts. To the extent that he is naïve, he is handicapped in his efforts to promote justice. God has given him his reason. It is his duty to use it in studying the political order.

6. Because the state can become tyrannical, the Christian acknowledges the right of rebellion, but he strives for a structure in which changes of government can be accomplished without violence. He does not ignore the problems of structure and system in his zeal to work for the more personal welfare of people. He knows that a faulty structure can frustrate justice. He realizes that when the structure of government prevents the people from having a voice in advising what the governing party should or should not do, and makes difficult the

discussion and debate of public issues, conditions or disorder are created in the very instrument that is supposed to preserve order. For this reason the Christian politician constantly analyzes the political structure and suggests changes that will remove the barriers to justice. His views reveal that he respects the government as God's instrument of order and realistically faces the corrupting presence of sin.

The Christian knows that man tends to exalt his own power to a place of dominating concern in his life and that the demonic forces are too powerful to be restrained completely by mortal man. Therefore, he seeks for the redemption of political life from outside the sphere of politics. He does not put complete faith in any form of government. He knows that justice will never be perfectly achieved by man. More than the humanist who believes in man's goodness, the Christian realizes the dangers of tyranny and man's helplessness to abolish evil by right thinking and strenuous work. He looks for the redemption of political life by the grace of Jesus Christ. *A Christian in Politics, pp. 30-32*

DJ: While we may take for granted today that the church must engage the world, it was not a common assumption among America's Lutherans, pre-World War II. The Augustana Synod was vigorous in its social missions, that is, its work in establishing hospitals, homes for the aged, inner-city missions and medical missions and schools abroad. Other Lutheran synods were engaged in similar works of mercy. However, Lutherans were slower to speak of the role of government in social welfare and world issues.

Robert Anderson, in an essay "The Awakening Social Consciousness of the Augustana Lutheran Church", recaps what historians were saying about the Lutheran Church in general: "When the Lutheran Church is mentioned, it is often done in a rather negative frame of reference to show the quietism, or inactivity, of the Lutherans in the field of social action. Reinhold Niebuhr well illustrates this when he writes in his book, *Does Civilization Need Religion?* 'Lutheranism is the Protestant way of despairing of the world and of claiming victory for the religious ideal without engaging in the world in combat.' Elsewhere he has said, 'Unfortunately, Lutheran piety at its best, is too pure to affect the world.'" *The Heritage of Augustana*, 2004. p. 154

Meanwhile, even as Esbj was still preparing for a life of leading the Church into engagement with the world, the Augustana Lutheran Synod itself was changing.

To document the change, Anderson quotes Abdel Wentz in his *Basic History of Lutheranism in America*:

Since World War 11, Lutheran social activities and pronouncements have entered new areas that would have seemed unapproachable a generation earlier. Lutherans have concerned themselves with Christian citizenship, international affairs, social security for old age, universal military training, the atomic and hydrogen bombs. The influence of church groups is now regularly exerted upon lawmaking bodies. At mid-century Lutherans are prepared to bear corporate witness to the power of the gospel as a leaven in social life.

Persons with Gustavus connections were leading the way in creating that new emphasis, even before the war. In 1938 Edgar Carlson, at that time a professor at Gustavus, wrote, *If War Comes*, which was a defense of Christian pacifism. Carlson's efforts were the beginning of what is now the Lutheran Peace Fellowship. He was not alone as there was much support within the Augustana Synod and in 1939, the Synod approved the Oxford Conference antiwar declaration. With war looming, Carlson raised support for Lutheran conscientious objectors in Civilian Public Service.

It is somewhat surprising that in 1944, at the height of America's support for the war, Carlson was elected by the Minnesota Conference of the Augustana Synod to head the College in St. Peter. This was undoubtedly due to the respect that Church and society had for Dr. Carlson. Carlson's contribution to pacificism, however, according to Anderson, was confined to his writings rather than in providing active leadership. Carlson continued all his days to raise the thoughtful questions. In 1964, he wrote a pamphlet, *Think On These Things*, for the Lutheran Peace Fellowship. *Lutheran Peace Fellowship 60th Anniversary Timeline.*

Foremost in rescuing Luther and the Reformation as the direct cause of quietism, was Carlson's *Reinterpretation of Luther*. In that 1949 book, Carlson analyzed forty years of research by Swedish scholars on the subject of Luther and government. Carlson's scholarly work also led to another significant book, *The Church and the Public Conscience*. In this 1956 work, Carlson laid the theological groundwork for the Church's concern for social action.

Esbjornson's Gustavus colleagues became a community of Biblical scholars, most of whom were concerned with social ethics. Esbj believed strongly in a college as a community of scholars in conversation. He benefited from the views of members in the then Christianity and Philosophy departments. A brief review of some of the personalities shows a common concern for theologically based social ethics.

George Forell taught philosophy at Gustavus from 1947-1956. Forell became identified with the ethic he discovered in Luther which was "faith active in love." He published a work by that same title in 1959. Esbj and Forell were colleagues and the Esbjornsons and the Forells were great friends. One can only imagine the encouragement the two men provided to one another in further developing their own thoughts about Christian social ethics.

George Hall was also in the Christianity Department when Esbj was hired at Gustavus. The Halls were, in the words of Esbj, "a peace-loving family, concerned about the poor and those less fortunate." The Halls and the Esbjornsons were all very close. George and Lorena had lost three teenaged children to a rare disease. Their surviving daughter, Camilla, was a social worker who got caught up in the radical movement of the Symbionese Liberation Army and died in a shoot-out with the Los Angeles police. George Hall, though grieved by his daughter's resort to violence, was compassionately understanding of her. Hall was quoted as saying at the time of her burial in Saint Peter, "The causes they were concerned about, ecology, air pollution and women's rights, are important to us all." News reports described Camilla as "a gentle warrior" and more of a "flower child rather than a revolutionary." The Halls poured their grief into hard work on behalf of other people. Esbjornson later established the George Hall prize in religion at Gustavus to honor his teacher, friend and colleague.

Emmer Engberg joined the Gustavus Christianity Department in 1954. Engberg was a political and theological liberal who also taught ethics. Engberg's ethics had been hammered out through years of parish ministry, especially in the racially diverse city of Chicago. His firsthand look at racism made him passionate about open housing and civil rights. Engberg was known for his outspokenness and excitability over issues. There was no shortage of conversation about political issues with Engberg on hand.

Arnold E. Carlson, brother to Edgar, was on the faculty from 1947 until 1955 which meant that he and Esbj worked side by side for five years. Though his field was systematic theology, Carlson also had strong social concerns, teaching ethics as well. Later, he devoted his doctoral dissertation to reviving Luther's unity of justification and sanctification, that is, the relationship of faith and ethics. The title is illustrative, *The Holy Spirit and The Neighbor's Need*. Toward the end of his life, Arnold Carlson was devoting his efforts to antinuclear campaigns.

Bernhard Erling joined the faculty in 1957. Erling was a systematic theologian and Biblical scholar with a strong social outlook that might best be characterized as "Swedish democratic socialism." Erling was and is a forceful proponent of the Christian duty to pay sufficient taxes to undergird the social fabric. Erling also wrote on issues of peace-making.

Richard Reusch, one of the more colorful professors, joined the faculty in 1954. He fought with the Cossacks during the revolution in Russia and then became a missionary in Tanzania. Reusch was best known for his passionate appeals in chapel on behalf of "zee babies in Africa." A biography of Reusch was recently completed by his student, Dan Johnson.

Clair Johnson came to Gustavus in 1958 as half-time chaplain and half-time on the faculty, eventually relinquishing his chaplaincy duties and teaching full time. Johnson taught church history and brought the historian's long view to the debates.

So we have a remarkable faculty engaged in theology, philosophy, Bible and social ethics in the 1950s. This faculty was presided over by the president of the College, **Dr. Edgar M. Carlson** who, as noted, was in the forefront of Lutheran theologians reinterpreting Luther and rediscovering the ethic of a "faith active in love." Those had to be exciting times with each personality providing Esbjornson with intellectual and spiritual companionship that solidified his interest in Biblical and social ethics. As the years passed, Esbj was blessed with many other faculty colleagues, from all departments, who debated social ethics, but the fellowship he found in his first years on the faculty set the direction for his life-long pursuit and study of the ancient question, "How, then, shall we live?"

Esbj had the opportunity to study with Union Theological Seminary's ethicist and church historian, H. Richard Niebuhr. The writings of Roman Catholic, Daniel McGuire were also influential. All of these persons taught him to think as an ethicist. He especially liked a quote from McGuire, "The bane of ethics is not the unanswered question, it is the unasked question." McGuire provided what he called reality questions to use in analyzing moral events and situations. McGuire described an ethicist: "It is true to say that every person is an ethicist in pursuit of moral value. The special task of the professional ethicist is to attempt to bring sensitivity, reflection, and method to the way in which his fellow human beings have learned to do, or stumbled into doing, ethics." McGuire, *Death by Choice*, 1974. p 77.

Many of Esbj's students in ethics classes will remember his stories of real life situations which seemed to pit one social good against another. They had to wrestle with how they would proceed to make decisions in highly ambiguous and complex problems. Ethics is not a simple task as the choice is not always about good and evil but rather about choices which are either the lesser of two evils or two competing claims which are both good/evil.

In such cases and in many of life's complexities, Esbj knew it was not enough to have knowledge, nor merely a system whereby one could think one's way to an ethical stance. He personally acknowledged his deep need for wrestling with these questions in the presence of God. Again and again, Esbj was thrown back on prayer and a reliance on guidance by the Holy Spirit. Even so, he was never absolutist in the stance he took on a particular issue. Nor did he stray from the practice of reading scripture. He was steeped in the law and the prophets and the ethic of Jesus. The questions of "who is my neighbor?" and "what do I owe the neighbor?" never left him.

As one looks at the courses Esbj taught over the years at Gustavus, many of them were based on relating religion and, especially, the Bible to the practical ethical situations young professionals would encounter day to day. In 1965, Gustavus Adolphus College inaugurated the now well-established and renowned Nobel Conference. The theme was "Genetics and the Future of Man." It was Edgar Carlson's intent that such a science-based conference would have a prominent theologian who could address the conference and respond to the scientific presentations. Paul Ramsey was the first such person to be invited to a Nobel Conference. Ramsey, a professor of Christian ethics at Princeton, was one of the leading Christian ethicists of the day. Bioethics was not yet a known term or a disciplinary field. According to Esbj, Ramsey credited that Nobel Conference with setting him down the path to becoming the premier "bioethicist" in the field. Esbj met Paul Ramsey at the conference and the two shared exciting new thoughts. Ramsey's presentations also inspired the Gustavus pre-med students who were in attendance. They came to Esbj and requested a course in medicine and ethics. Esbj agreed as he saw the need of both premeds and nursing students for reflection on the ethics of medicine. The following is his course description as it appeared in the college catalog of courses.

> **Religion 442. Ethics and Medicine.** Juniors and above. Ethical perspectives are applied to the diagnosis of the moral issues that confront people involved in medical situations: What is health? What are the responsibilities of the healing professions in relation to the adequacy of the medical care system, the problems that arise at the beginning and end of life, and the issues posed by the increasing power to fabricate human life and manipulate human behavior and consciousness? Students are expected to be prepared by a variety of readings to carry the initiative in the weekly discussion and to formulate their views on various issues in written form.

He believed that our many business majors needed the same opportunity to wrestle thoughtfully with ethical issues they would face.

> **Religion 443. Ethics and Economics.** Juniors and above. The application of ethical process to a diagnosis of optional economic theories and business ethics. The historical relations between economic activity and religion will be explored, along with current economic issues and future prospects. Style: case studies, role playing, use of novels, guest interviews, basic literature.

In a 1985 paper, "Why Study Ethics?" Esbj wrote, "Ethics is a disciplined study of human choices and the social settings of those choices. It is a diagnostic process. It has to be disciplined, careful--much like a physician's diagnosis of a patient. Morality or codes of ethics are formed because humans so often experience situations in which choices must be made. Our codes provide some guidance in making choices. I hope an ethics course would help someone attain an increasing awareness of moral experience, more sensitivity to recognize moral issues and to analyze those situations and to make sound selection of moral beliefs that can stand up under the tensions of living in a changing society. I hope an ethics course would help the persons learn the skill of making applications of one's analyses in the process of imagining possible options for policy or actions and give the person more confidence in making decisions."

A student, Rich Koglin, said of his course, "At first I was dismayed because the course (Ethics and Medicine)--and he--lacked the firm structure of the science courses with which I was familiar. But I soon saw that this lack of structure was purposeful---that Esbj viewed ethics not as a textbook subject, but as a process by which one weighed and considered conflicting values."

Esbjornson's work was increasingly moving to ethical concerns. However, he grounded all of his work and his freedom to confront every question in his confidence in God. He spelled this out in a lengthy theological treatise: "A Theology for the Conversation with Science and Technology." A short excerpt is printed here.

RE: Luther helped us to create the modern age because his rediscovery of the Gospel liberated many people from the worst tyranny there is--the fear that God is against humanity and that humans are condemned now and through eternity if they do not please God. Over many centuries a complex ecclesiastical system designed to deal with that fear had developed, and it was so pervasive that the land was filled with penitential prayers, shrines, churches, holy days and clergy of various kinds. Faith in Christ as Lord who revealed God's love for sinners in his life, death and resurrection liberated humanity. In his own words Luther put it simply: "When you know that you have through Christ a good and gracious God who will forgive your sins and remember them no more, and are now a child of eternal blessedness, a lord over heaven and earth with Christ, then you have nothing more to do than to go about your business and serve your neighbor." It was a freedom to live in the world boldly and in the practical service in the various stations of society.

At about the same time the scientific revolution was beginning, and the issues it would raise were not yet clear. Modern sciences have presented formidable and sometimes devastating challenges to traditional ideas that were taken for granted at the time of the Reformation. Astronomy gave humanity an immense universe in which the Earth was no longer the center but a very small speck in a solar system within a minor galaxy. Biology, geology and paleontology gave us a picture of the development of organisms over a very long span of time as an explanation of the appearance and disappearance of an incredible variety of species and for the changes in the Earth's forms. Physics and molecular biology have made us aware of the basic and common structures of all forms of life and our connections with animals and even simple life forms such as bacteria. Psychology has given us a glimpse of the depths of mental processes operating beyond the reach of consciousness and often beyond its control. Sociology and cultural anthropology have placed beliefs and customs into a social context and thus have relativized what we would like to believe are universal matters. Ecology has undermined our sense of dominance over the environments that sustain us and our confidence in an ever-expanding productivity as a basis for prosperity. And now recent developments in medical science have required us to question former beliefs about the limits of human powers to shape the very substance of life and to control death.

We cannot in good conscience sidestep the issues presented by the sciences. The challenge will not go away, and few people are ready to reject all the technological applications that have brought benefits as well as costs.

If we are engaged in a helpful and creative conversation about the biomedical revolution and the issues it raises, we should include the revolutionary implications of the story of God that has created and shaped the Church.

That story inspires a primal belief: *The most splendid, strong and sacred reality in human experience is the relationship with a gracious God who creates, redeems and sanctifies our lives and our worlds.* Death is not our final master or reality, nor is life, nor are the principalities and powers that bear down upon us in our life stories. A gracious God is.

DJ: On this premise, Esbj believed, the Church should rest its confidence in entering into dialogue about things uncertain, futures unknowable and multiple threats to life itself. God is creator, redeemer and sanctifier.

Esbj and Amos:

DJ: In several different sermons preached by Esbj, he spoke about Amos, how he first met Amos, the prophet, and how Amos transformed his thinking again and again. From a sermon in Christ Chapel in the year 2000:

RE: Amos had some harsh judgment to say about war crimes, cruelty and injustice. His judgments were not just against individuals but the injustices of the systems of domination. He called women cows, because they pressured their husbands to bring more income home so they could have more of what they wanted. He had harsh words about judges and courts in his time and would have about systems of justice in our time for failing to be just to the powerless while favoring the powerful. He would be hard on the elite who are rich and powerful and who love the fast life in their fancy houses and clubs but do not care for the suffering of the oppressed and poor. He had harsh things to say to priests and the sounds of their solemn assemblies, who were more concerned about right rituals than righteous minds, hearts and actions.

Amos first came into my life in the fall of 1941, the days before Pearl Harbor. I was doing something ordinary for a student--working on an assignment for a class in prophetic literature at the seminary in Rock Island. As I struggled to understand the message of Amos, the seminary chorus was singing in the chapel in the upper floor over the library. "O God, our help in ages past, our hope for years to come." That powerful music merged with the powerful poetry of Amos. I experienced a transformation. God was more than my personal Lord and Savior, my family's God, the God of my people. God is the Lord of all nations, all people. I had not understood God in that way before. From that moment on I could not understand God as anything less than the Lord of all nations. I also saw salvation differently. It was no longer the salvation of my soul so that I would make it through this life until I die and go to heaven. It was the salvation for public life, for the systems of government, economic life, human relations. Righteousness was not just a matter of personal life, but of public life. Justice was not getting even for someone who wronged me or someone I loved. It was no longer a matter of my rights to fair reward for what I had done. It was a matter of concern for the lives of the poor, the oppressed. This view of things is found all through the Bible. It changed my way of thinking, feeling and acting. It was not a total change, for I had a long way to go, and I am still on it.

That was not the last time that Amos came into my life. He came to me at Gustavus in the early '60s. My class in Bible brought a modern Amos into our panel discussion. He was Michael Harrington. His book, *The Other America*, was about the poor in our own country. Amos came again when I was teaching a course in the urban church. I took students to Milwaukee's inner city and met a Lutheran who left a career in real estate to become the director of a program to provide low cost housing for the urban poor, not his own people, for most of them were black. He, like Amos, knew the facts about the need for housing for the poor and he had a passion for justice.

A few days ago, Amos came again, this time to the Nobel Conference on globalization in the person of a man named Sach and his lecture on the economy as it affects the poorest of the poor. He had a vast knowledge of conditions and deep passion for justice.

A couple of Sundays ago, Amos came in an editorial in the Sunday Tribune about Africa and AIDS, a passionate appeal for our country to do something. Amos keeps coming and coming. Since that day in 1941, Amos has come to me again and again, gradually transforming my life.

Christ Chapel, October, 2000

DJ: In a 1988 sermon, Esbj spoke about another transforming experience with Amos:

RE: Some years ago I was in Jerusalem, less than a dozen miles from Tekoa, in the wilderness of Judea where Amos lived long ago. I was a member of a travel seminar for teachers of Bible. We visited the memorial to the six million Jews slaughtered in the Nazi death camps. Walking by the wall-sized photos of scenes from the camps of emaciated, empty faces, and piles of corpses was a jolting experience. Then I came upon a glass display case containing only one shoe. A child's shoe. A child gassed in the ovens of Auschwitz. That's all that was left. One shoe.

I went outside. I stood in stunned silence. I could not speak, but I could pray silently.

And I vowed, before God, not just any god, but the God of Amos and Jesus, my father's God, my mother's God, that I would never tolerate cruelty to anyone, not violence of language, not physical violence. Amos was there that day.

Amos came again in the writings of Karen Lebacqz in her book, *Justice in an Unjust World*. In that work, Lebacqz said, "If the story is not told, justice dies." I knew when I read those words what I must do whenever and wherever I can. And I am doing it now--telling the story of God, whose name cannot be separated from the word justice."

Christ Chapel November 28, 1988

A Poem: **Amos Comes to Saint Peter**

Woe to you who are at leisure in the College
　　And feel secure on the hill
Who live in comfortable, lovely houses
　　On quiet suburban streets,
Who feast on Grade A sirloin
　　Broiled over charcoal
And washed down with Hills Brothers'
　　coffee,
Who listen to the free music on Minnesota Public
　　Radio
And watch sex and violence on television,
But are not grieved over the ruin of the
　　Families in poverty
And ignore the "Other America"
　　In the urban ghettoes!

Woe to you who go to Trinity and transgress,
　　And to First Lutheran and
　　Multiply transgressions
　　And in Christ Chapel double all your Sins.

Beware, I hate, I despise your festivals,
　　I take no delight in your solemn
　　　　Worship services,

30

Even though you multiply them by two
    During Lent
And fill the world with your hymns and
    anthems.

Let justice roll down like waters,
    And righteousness like a mighty stream.

Because you trample upon the poor
    By your tolerance of injustice,
You shall not long dwell in your houses of
    Hewn Kasota stone
Nor in your houses by the lakes.

Because the righteous are sold for silver,
    And the needy for a pair of shoes
Because they that trample on the heads of the
    Poor are not brought to justice,
Behold, the days are coming upon you
    When you shall be taken away with hooks
And the last of you with fish-hooks
As the man at the city dump rescues from the
    Rats the leftovers of your affluent Homes.
So shall the people of suburbia be rescued,
    With the corner of a couch and a part
    Of a bed.

    – Esbj's paraphrase of Amos, Chapters 4-6

Esbj speaking at Riverbend, 1969

Chapter Three
Community:
Gustavus, St. Peter and Riverbend

DJ: As has been cited earlier, Esbj had a strong conviction about a college as a community of scholars and he guarded every expression of community. His definition of community included "the Hill," the neighborhood, the town, the church and the wider community.

Community Worship

Esbj valued daily chapel for the opportunity to pray, sing and hear the Word. However, he also saw the great contribution chapel made to creating community. This was especially true when chapel attendance was compulsory and everyone shared the experience. When Christ Chapel was built in 1962, the College no longer required chapel attendance. Esbj affirmed the change. Students and faculty who now went to chapel were there because they wanted to be and, therefore, a deeper attitude of reverence was obvious. It was the end of "chapel pranks." Even as he rejoiced in the enhanced quality of the worship experience, nevertheless, he mourned the absence of a daily event which brought the entire community together. Subsequent chapters will tell the story of Esbj's strong advocacy of the practice of daily worship on the Gustavus campus.

Coffee and Community at the Canteen.

Esbj was an active participant in the stimulating coffee table conversations in the canteen. When Esbj began his teaching at Gustavus, the canteen was located in the basement of Uhler Hall. The faculty table was a place for both quiet conversations and boisterous arguments. The topics were typically about ideas, film, theater, sports, national politics, religion or the latest controversies related to policies of the Gustavus administration. Students were often invited to join the conversation. Later, in the Johnson Student Union, the faculty coffee table continued. If students sat at the table, it was also true that faculty occasionally peeled away from the table to sit with students.

In *The Gustavus Quarterly* (Fall 2000), Steve Benson, '63, director of the Osher Lifelong Learning Institute (OLLI) at the University of Minnesota remembers the "roundtable" conversations in the canteen. "That was learning," stated Benson, "the most stimulating learning experiences were not formal classes, but the conversation at the roundtable." There he and others had the chance to interact with a number of faculty and staff persons and to argue and debate. Benson's work with OLLI seeks to recapture that interactive kind of learning in the courses and classes he designs for "lifelong" learners.

Esbj was a regular at the table and he was steadfast in his opposition to proposals for a separate faculty lounge or dining room. He wanted to be accessible to students even on a break and he wanted them included in the conversations.

The Neighborhood Community of Valley View

Following World War II and into the early '50s, many faculty and staff persons were building homes. This was made possible, in part, by generous loans to them from the *Greater Gustavus Fund*.

To help meet the mortgage, families rented out their basement areas to students who wanted to live off campus. Valley View was then a new development and many faculty and staff (as well as a few merchants and professionals) lived in what was to become a tightly knit community. Gus and Evelyn Young, Chet and Marian Johnson, Vic and Betty Gustafson, Floyd and Bea Martinson, Ross and Lavinia Bloomquist, Don and Gene Lund, Kyle and Doris Montague, Ellery and Aileen Peterson, and Don and Marlys Slarks were among the Gustavus people who lived in Valley View at the same time. Neighborhood picnics, gatherings after sporting and cultural events, and back and forth socializing kept the conversations going. There was no isolation of department from department.

Campus Social Life As Community Builder

Esbj loved campus life and took an active interest in most of it. He wrote about the campus love affairs, student gripes about the required Christianity courses, required chapel, and the food service. Esbj wrote of one campus tradition that helped build community, the annual "Faculty Follies."

RE: Faculty Follies, performed in the dreary late winter days of March, did much to diffuse the tensions and the stress of the students and faculty. Faculty acted the role of clowns and made fun of students. The students packed the house for the event. I have vivid memories of those Follies, such as Alfredella Noleen (from the Home Economics Department) pursuing the rotund and dignified Classics professor, Bertil Larson, fleeing down rows of students in their seats. We portrayed student couples smooching in front of Wahlstrom Hall before the doors were locked. We re-created another scene in front of Rundstrom where the often dateless senior girls lived. There was not a single couple in sight, only a large cutout car with smoke pouring from its windows which let them all know that we knew the car was the girls' smoking place behind Rundstrom. The football games in the stadium and the basketball games in Myrum Memorial Fieldhouse were other events that bonded us all into a community.

DJ: One of the endearing qualities admired by students was his humanity. Esbj enjoyed being caricatured and could laugh at himself. When a new pope was being elected in Rome, Cameron Johnston '60 drew a poster that declared "Esbj for Pope"and posted it in the student union. A faculty person, not wanting Bob embarrassed, took it down and gave it to Esbj. He loved it and kept it as a trophy.

The Local Church Community

Esbjornson's involvement at First Lutheran Church, Saint Peter, also put him in contact with other faculty as they worked together in church activities. It was yet another arena for the conversation. It also put faculty in contact with townspeople and farmers and kept them in touch with other perspectives and got them out of any ivory tower. Still another avenue was his service as pastor for several years to Bethany Lutheran Church, Judson, which allowed Esbj the privilege of addressing his sermons to a congregation different in make-up from the students, faculty and staff at Gustavus.

The Community of the Wider Church

Esbj was an active participant in the conference, district, and synodical gatherings of the church. Many letters from pastors expressed gratitude for the way that Esbjornson and many of his colleagues, especially Clair Johnson and Bernhard Erling, attended and made their voices heard in pastoral conferences. Again, it was a demonstration that these professors did not want to do their academic work apart from conversations with the pastors and lay members of the Lutheran congregations supporting Gustavus. As such, he and the others were wonderful ambassadors to the wider Church.

Saint Peter and Beyond

If ever there was a town-gown distinction, Esbj and others bridged that gap with their community activism. St. Peter was not just where he lived; it was where he found community. That he viewed himself as a citizen with obligations was also evident in the roles he played in community service, whether as adviser on the ethics board of the Minnesota Regional Treatment Center, the board of the St. Peter Food Co-Op, or as a volunteer with Meals on Wheels. He found delight in being part of community and contributing to it.

Esbj As Community Activist: The Riverbend Association

"Who would expect 'Riverbend' to emerge out of a department of religion?" Letter, 1983 Edgar M. Carlson, former president (1944-1968), Gustavus Adolphus College.

With the arrival of Gustavus' 4-1-4 academic calendar came many opportunities for innovative travel courses for Gustavus students and professors. Esbj

seized the opportunity and created "The Urban Church" seminar. In cooperation with the progressive Ecumenical Institute of Chicago, Esbj located the program in the heart of urban struggles with poverty, crime, violence and racism.
The goal was to expose students to the urban scene and the study programs that
were addressing those challenges.

It was a popular program, and by all accounts, very successful. Several students found their lifework as a result of that program. However, there was a
larger spin-off from the venture. As Esbj and the students studied and experienced Chicago's inner core and community leadership responses to it, Esbj
began to ask the question about the issues facing rural America and, especially,
the Minnesota River Valley. How can the community of Saint Peter and the
other small towns up and down the river, come together to address the pressing
issues of the time?

New ideas frequently have more than one source for their inspiration and
conception. At the second annual Nobel Conference held at the college in 1966,
Orville Freeman, former Minnesota governor and then secretary of agriculture,
gave a principal address on the theme of "Managing our Environment." Freeman set out the premise on which the Riverbend Association was formed. Esbj's
notes record what Freeman said:

If the present trend in the placement of our people continues, there will be
just as many of us in 216 cities by 1985 as there were in the entire nation in
1960......more people bunched in great cities, more urban sprawl on the edges
of cities, more filth, traffic, etc... We can make a valuable contribution to the
future well-being of our nation: creating and maintaining more opportunities
for people to live good lives *where the space is: rural America*. Rural America has
not only exported food but its people...bright, able youngsters find decreasing
opportunity in rural areas so they move to the cities. Only if we raise the quality
of life in the countryside can this *forced* migration be halted.

DJ: "His statements are germinating in my mind," wrote Esbj. The result was
a paper he produced which became an invitation to citizens of the four county
"bend of the river" area to come together to talk about common concerns.

RE: Is it possible that the people of this area can create a new concept of
living, a style that combines in a new, exciting pattern the values of both rural
and urban life? A *rurban* style? An alternative to the dying small towns and
congested urban centers? It is not too late to plan and work for a Riverbend Alternative: Rurbanity, something refreshing, challenging enough to attract people
and make them want to live in our area, something so good it is so superb that
we can have a sense of pride and accomplishment rather than a sense of being
victims of what happens to us and our area.

DJ: Forty persons responded and came to the meeting. There was a consen-
sus to form the Riverbend Steering Committee. Hearings were held in sev-

eral towns. This gave rise to the Riverbend Association. Riverbend involved farmers, merchants, educators, lawyers, judges, clergy, physicians, homemakers, elected officials, captains of industry and agri-business. Bob Moline, Gustavus geography professor, commenting 40 years later said, "There was indeed much discussion about existing regional organizations like the Metropolitan Council in the Twin Cities area and we wondered why that concept should not be applied to the more rural/small town parts of the state; we'd be populist, more grass roots. Esbj was the force and his leadership was recognized in his election as chair." Esbj threw his energies into this and drew many of his students into the project as well.

In 1968, the "Planning for Rurbania--1988" conference drew 600 persons. Speakers addressed issues of economic development, the care of the environment, urban design, the role of religion, the family farm, the future of education and historic site preservation. The person most responsible for Minnesota's newest planned community of Jonathan was enlisted as a resource. He asked, "Could the same kind of planning be done for much older and established communities?"

The steering committee followed up on the symposium and formed 12 commissions to consider the topics to be addressed: Water and Resources, Economic Development, Agriculture and Agri-industry, Education, Outdoor Recreation, Population Trends and Human Relations, Religious Life, Historical Sites, Natural Resources Inventory and Conservation, Intergovernmental Relations, Art and Culture, and Communications.

The goal was, according to Esbj, "to have an interrelating of counties for a comprehensive planning project." Professor Bob Moline, who worked with Esbj on River Bend, said, "He is a holistic thinker, interested in connections, in synergistic effects, absolutely taken with John Muir's observation that everything is connected to everything else."

Ever the ethicist and the futurist, Esbj defined "rurbanity" as "an alternative to rural decline and urban danger, a lifestyle that unites such cherished rural virtues as cooperation, hospitality and personal responsibility with new urban traits such as careful and skillful planning, a cosmopolitan tolerance for human differences, a willingness to be comprehensive rather than narrowly restricted in thinking and innovative in approaching problems; it is an attitude that combines delight in and respect for our natural environment and respect for and responsibility for man's technology.

He referred to the commissions as scouting parties of the association, like those who went ahead of the pioneers' wagon trains--scouts who went to see what lay ahead, both in terms of dangers and opportunities.

Ken E. Berg, of the *Mankato Free Press*, wrote that the role of Riverbend has been that of a "catalyst in simply getting together the mix of common people and common interests which reflects broad loyalty to a region and not to the narrow confines of one town or another within that region."

Berg continued, "Riverbend took off like a bird, as it were, in the years of vacuum between the presumed end of civic isolationism in 1966 and passage of the Regional Development Act of 1969. The unique (in Minnesota) self-help planning concept initially drew wide attention and support; rallies were called and rave notices were written and dispatched in all directions. The impending receipt of federal assistance ('without money there is no program, and without a program there is no function') seemed a foregone conclusion amid the accolades which inferred more promise than hint."

The anticipated funding never arrived. The wind went out of Riverbend's sails. The organization continued until Esbj's own energies needed to be directed toward the development of new courses to meet new needs of his students. When Esbj resigned the chairmanship, the organization quietly faded.

Berg offered a reason why Riverbend never went from vision to implementation. "No doubt the arrival of the formal Region Nine authority nipped Riverbend's aspirations of functionalism in the bud. It is reasonable to argue, I suppose, that the present regionalism setup makes redundancy of Riverbend and of Riverbend's high-minded goals."

So what did Riverbend actually accomplish? At the very least, it got many people talking together about common problems, empowering citizens to shape their own collective future rather than to passively accept what others planned for them. It shaped a mindset of "regionalism" which has only grown since the Riverbend was formed. In a letter to Esbj, Orville Freeman stated that the biggest challenge would be "creating an area-wide feeling of community such as people now feel for their own town."

Bob Moline describes a successful intervention of plans by the U.S. Corps of Engineers to build a series of dams on the Minnesota River that would have controlled floods. "One of the dams would have created a floodpool that would have covered most of Garden City. Needless to say, the Garden City folks were not happy. To the Corps' credit, it decided to hold its hearing on the dam in the gym of the high school in Garden City. I assembled a small committee and we had great conversations. We prepared a comment about the dam and submitted it to the Corps. I prepared the comment and we attended the packed meeting. Many others felt as we did that trying to control floods is the wrong task. The real goal should be to work on ways to reduce flood damages. When one asks that question, a whole different set of alternative solutions emerge. The Corps dropped their dams-on-the-Minnesota proposal and we've heard nothing about that since. The idea of participating in this specific regional planning project grew out of the Riverbend concept."

Riverbend was also an example of professors who refused to live in an ivory tower of ideas without having to get one's hands dirty in the messiness of politics, self-interest and conflict over differing visions. It also gave Esbjornson case studies for his classes on Church and Society. Students met with community leaders, and analyzed commission reports according to outlined criteria. Several of his students took the reports and wrote an extensive paper on what reforms were needed on every level of government in order to create the good life for a maximum number of its citizens. Utopian to some, the paper was a student exercise in thinking together about some of the most vexing problems of society.

William Robertz, Gustavus Speech professor, wrote, "Mr. Esbjornson's presentation of the Riverbend Association admirably manifests ideas in action. His conception of 'rurbania' denies the stereotyped effete intellectual and recalls Emerson's ideal of *The American Scholar* for whom 'action….is essential, without it thought can never ripen into truth.'"

In a letter to Esbj upon the occasion of Esbj's retirement, Edgar M. Carlson observed: "Who would have thought that Riverbend Association would have come out of the Department of Religion?" The answer, as Carlson well knew, lay in the fact that the department of religion had one of the most creative and active minds in the person of Robert Esbjornson.

Esbj at Gustavus Graduation, 1996.

Chapter Four

The Christian as Scholar in the Gustavus Tradition

DJ: As noted earlier, some colleagues occasionally made the statement that "Esbj was not a serious scholar." On the face of it, the statement makes a valid point. Esbj, apparently, lacked the motivation or discipline to seek the PhD that would have put him on an equal level with others in the faculty. He, himself, wrote that he "lacked the credentials of a scholar." However, by other criteria, Esbj was most certainly scholarly. He was constantly reading, arguing, writing, and investigating. His was an active mind. He sought not to become the expert, for example, on "ethics and medicine." He read widely in the field of medicine, and then relied on the knowledge of others as he shaped the ethical questions to be asked of those in the field.

Another trait necessary to scholarship is what Esbj called, "honesty before piety." He articulated the dilemma of how to teach Bible to students whose faith might be shaken by the critical studies of the holy book. He wrote:

RE: The claim of truth on me became very evident during the 17 years I taught courses in the Bible. The conventional wisdom widely proclaimed among Lutherans (and others) was that the Bible is the Word of God, an infallible guide for belief and behavior. Taken at face value, that belief inspired devout study of the Bible. However, the claim of truth carries the responsibility of teaching and publishing what we discover in the study of the *Bible as it is.*

As I worked with the biblical literature and the findings of biblical scholars, it soon became clear that the literature was not so simple. The books were written originally as responses to and interpretations of specific historical situations. They were complex literary documents, containing a variety of literary forms ranging from personal letters to long sagas originally passed along orally, from poetry to ideologically constructed histories, law and skeptical literature of sages. The books also had a variety of theological and moral teachings that made comparisons necessary.

For scholars teaching religion at a liberal arts college of the Church, there is an inescapable tension between two important tasks-- that of guiding students toward a mature faith and instilling in them a devotion to truth. How can we teach ideas that may be a challenge to cherished opinions in such a way that it is enlightening and nurturing at the same time? I quote from Edgar Carlson:

It must be recognized that education in general and colleges in particular have an independent basis for existence which is rooted in the mind's quest for truth and in the nature of the learning process. It cannot allow itself to be regarded solely as the instrument of any other "order", be it the family, the Church, or the State. It transmits the cultural heritage from one generation to another but in doing so it applies the critical apparatus of sound scholarship to that heritage. It interprets the present and explores the unknown with all the resources available to it and with a mind that is not predetermined by any obligation except its faithfulness to truth. This is its particular and distinctive service.

This means that the quest for truth must be genuine. Those to whom the Church entrusts the quest for truth must be free to pursue it. Since the function of a liberal arts college includes the critical analysis of the culture which it transmits and the continuous exploration of new fields of knowledge and the implications of new discoveries, it (the Church) must expect that its own teaching will be subject to that same critical analysis. Indeed, this is part of what it is paying for. Edgar M. Carlson, 1962 essay

DJ: Often, Esbjornson was invited to give an orientation to new faculty about the church-related dimensions of Gustavus. One such talk was titled *"Curiosity, Care and Contemplation."*

RE: Today I shall speak as a scholar about a scholar's work. I do not belong to the guild. Only those who carry the union card, a Ph.D., can belong as full members. But I believe I am scholarly. I may not have all of the credentials of a scholar, but I think I have the characteristics--if not all, at least three, and they are basic.

Curiosity.

Humans are inherently curious. We ask, "What is that?" "Why is it here?" "What does it mean?" Our minds are restless, insatiable in the hunger to know and understand. Curiosity is generated by something beyond ourselves as thinking beings. The "something" might be as distant as the birth of the remotest galaxy or as intimately close as the neural patterns of the human brain, as foreign as the ruins in a Central American jungle or as familiar as our own thought processes. We are curious about the worlds we inhabit and about ourselves in those worlds.

I am curious, too, about religion. What is there about humans that is so basic in them, so strong, that they create religious stories, rituals, beliefs, moral rules, communities? I am utterly fascinated by the nature of religious experience, how it is different from and related to other experiences such as moral experience, or the love of beauty, or the devotion of a scientist, or the craft of a statesman? Why do people pray to a god who lets them die even though they have beseeched for life, or who apparently cannot or will not stop the untimely death of a child or a wife?

What is going on in all this? This very ambiguous, elusive aspect we call the spirit, the soul? Where faith and doubt meet, where hope and despair vie for dominance? Where hate and love meet head on?

I hear a soft voice calling through the noise of ambiguous, puzzling contradictions.

'Robert, take off your shoes. You are standing on holy ground.' So I do. I take off my prior opinions and prejudices. I shed beliefs I thought were safely true. I allow myself to stand as naked as a babe in the presence of something so attractive that I cannot but investigate. To that something over There, beyond me, that Other.

Curiosity must come with a strong sense of respect for what is there, for truth. It is curiosity that drives scholars to exploration, it is truth that compels us to teach and publish what we learn. We must be faithful to what we learn. We must tell the truth as it becomes clear to us. If we do not tell what we know, if we suppress genuine evidence or distort it to fit into previous views, we are traitors to our own work. We are confronted by realities so imperious, so strongly present that we become stalkers. We are drawn, like Moses, to our bushes that burn but are not consumed. We become inquirers, then investigators devising the most appropriate ways of investigating what we have found. There is an inviolable hardness about the realities that move in on us that makes it objectionable or at least uncomfortable for us to twist the truth to fit our own needs and aims. Truth moves in on us with a force that shatters neat theories and models with a relentless power over which we have no full control.

Caring Community

There is another characteristic of scholarly life. Humans are social animals who cannot get along without human connections, and sometimes cannot get along within them. Human relations are ambiguous affairs in which cooperation and conflict seem to persist together. A college is a community of shared tasks and beliefs but also an arena of conflicting views in which it is hard for one to be dominant. Living in such a place draws us into a drama in which we care for and about one another, and yet get into power struggles for dominance. Conflict and confrontation are facts of life in the scholarly life. They are supposed to take place in a reasonable and polite way, but it is not rare that the gloves come off and the struggle gets rather rough. Being a college connected with the Church and influenced by the Christian heritage, caring is an obligation that mitigates, even if it does not entirely eliminate, conflict. Scholarly work is both very lonely and solitary work at times and also a joint venture, and there is plenty of both at Gustavus. We are an academic community, not just a collection of individuals who happen to occupy adjacent spaces. No one has a claim on all the truth, but everyone has a glimpse of the whole. Respect for each other

43

starts with humility about ourselves. Intellectual arrogance is a deadly sin, challenged only by being candid with each other and held in check only if we truly care about each other.

Contemplation

Contemplation starts in and then goes beyond scholarly orientation. By contemplation I mean the stance and act of giving attention to what is transcendent in human experience. It may well be that it is grounded in the fearful experience of human contingency and powerlessness, in the experience of the unknown that seems to defy adequate explanation and symbolization. It may have been generated in the encounter of forces beyond human ability to master, generated in weakness and not strength. But the contemplative impulse, once it is awakened by experience and nurtured by religious practices, takes on a power of its own and becomes inherently valuable. People may begin to worship out of some need external to the relationship with the transcendent, the god, but they do not long continue in that vein. The hunger and thirst for God become compelling enough to generate the stance and acts of contemplation. Worship is essentially paying attention to God, to the Source, or whatever metaphor we may find expressive of the experience of the transcendent.

From this perspective of time in my life, near the end of my career, what we call "chapel" is the one feature that has provided continuity and shaped the character of the College. The rhythms of worship go on year after year. They are the pulse of the Gustavus heart. The hymns, the scriptures readings, the intercessions and petitions, the preaching give the College a quality of life that comes from beyond itself. The steady beat of prayers was going on here before I was born and will continue after I die.

Gustavus Traditions

DJ: Sometime in the late '60s or early '70s, Esbj was chosen to give the faculty speech to students during freshman orientation. The theme was "The Traditions of Gustavus." This edited speech reveals the whole picture of Gustavus and its traditions. Esbj lifts up three traditions that must not be betrayed. The speech is both an interesting look at traditions that have been discarded and traditions that live. This speech reveals the heart of Esbj and his core convictions.

RE: Traditions that change at Gustavus

Traditions are a living and powerful influence in the life of a community. Perhaps they are more important than the individuals. They certainly outlast individuals and do much to shape individuals. Some traditions die, either because they have outlived their significance or use and others because people dropped them, betrayed them.

Here are a few examples of how traditions change. The rising bell is at 5:45 a.m. ---in the 1880s. Now the tradition is:

Get in classes from ten to one, if you want any time for fun.

It is the custom to go for a hike in the country on Sunday to a hospitable farmer for a good meal as a change from the college board. That was in the 1880s. Now:

Holiday House and Pizza Village provide you with excellent midnight fillage.

Each student staying at the College Hall (the name for Old Main, years ago) must take his turn chopping wood for the stoves in the rooms. Today:

Fires in dormitories are forbidden, be sure to keep your appliances hidden.

Once upon a time there was this rule: No young man shall be seen walking with a young woman unless they are engaged or have the President's permission. The effect of this was twofold: walks where couples would not be seen and a sudden rise in the number of engaged couples. Nowadays:

No boys allowed in Wahlstrom hallways. Take your gals out on lonely byways.

It has always cost money to go to Gustavus. In the 1890s tuition was $20 a year. In 1940 Sunday dinner cost 22 cents at the cafeteria. Today:

Loan me a twenty, roomy, my pal. I've got a date with my little gal.

The Tradition of Gustie Spirit and Friendliness

Gustavus is a community of people who not only study together, but live together and play together. It is a tradition to refer to the Gustie spirit. It is hard to define but not to experience. Friendliness is a large sized ingredient in the Gustie spirit. You will find camaraderie here, the personal touch. In fact, before you know it your roommate has touched you for five dollars, and you have a hard time getting anything but a busy signal when you call Wahlstrom; and you will be initiated into one of the most famous traditions of all, the Canteen conversations around tables that can hold more people and dirty coffee cups than any in the world.

Some of us think Gustavus has a tradition of beautiful girls, too. In fact, we have so many of them that we cannot settle for just a Homecoming Queen. We also have to elect a Frosh Queen, St. Lucia Queen, Frost Queen, Viking Queen, Svea Queen of May Day--and just for contrast, the Ugly Man election. There is a tradition of falling in love with a wonderful Gustavus girl or that Gustavus guy. You might, too.

The traditional symbol of friendliness at Gustavus is Hello Walk that crosses the front of the campus on the brow of the hill. Once it was the only walk and shorter. Now, it has several rivals and is nearly a half-mile long. You have not begun to live until you have walked it from Valley View Hall to the Art Barn for an eight o'clock class in January with the wind out of the northwest at 30 miles and the temperature at minus 10. There is an apocryphal story about a girl who started from South Hall one morning to go to a history class in the Classroom Annex. The wind was so strong that by the time of the bell she was no farther than Vickner Hall, so she went to class there and soon transferred her major to English.

In whatever activity you engage you will find the Gustie spirit--whether band practice, choir rehearsal, committee meetings, field trips, frats and sororities, athletics, or student government. If you came here hoping to find the personal rather than the impersonal, a family spirit rather than an institutional formality, you will not be disappointed. But in order to experience this you must be true to the Gustavus tradition of friendliness yourself; you must enter into the spirit of the occasion.

The Tradition of Scholarship

Gustavus is not just a community of friendly people. It is a college, a community of scholars united in the quest for truth, responsible for a heritage, subject to the disciplines of study, reading, research and rehearsal which the pursuing and professing of truth require.

This campus is primarily the setting not for romance, games, parties, prayer meetings or playing, but for study. There will be times when you will find that the very friendliness and camaraderie of this campus will make it hard for you to study. You will long for solitude and silence, for the chance to be alone with a book and to think. Privacy is not easy to come by. Our modern life pattern too readily violates the individual's right of privacy and solitude. The pressure of the boys who want a fourth hand for poker or the girls who want a fourth for bridge, the crowded and noisy conditions of the dormitory, the lack of space in the library will not make it easy for you, but if you do not become adjusted to the Gustavus tradition of study you will betray what this college stands for. If you came to Gustavus primarily to play football, meet a man, shelter your morals or piety or to have a blast-- you will be unadjusted here--one who betrays rather than delivers a Gustie tradition.

Gustavus in intent on educating you--drawing you out of yourself into a community of scholars, helping you experience the rare excitement of exploring new ideas and phenomena, opening your eyes to new worlds.

There is one other academic tradition which everyone hopes you will not betray while you are here. That is *the tradition of integrity, academic honesty.* There is no crime or immorality that is more heinous at a college than cheating. Cheating is a blow to the heart of the academic task, because it is a denial of the very truth to which we are committed to foster. The pursuit of truth and cheating are irreconcilable.

46

The Tradition of Liberal Arts

Gustavus is a special kind of college. We call it a liberal arts college. This is a very special tradition that can be characterized in many ways, but one thing is constant. At this college there is a tradition of honoring curiosity about everything. Gustavus respects the human trait of wanting to learn for no other reason than because to know is a delight in itself. Gustavus wants to encourage and train this natural curiosity, for in doing so it helps each person become more truly a human being. Gustavus wants to transmit to you the precious heritage of the past and to train you to probe the frontiers of the unknown. No walls are erected around sacrosanct topics--religion, the Vietnam War, the capitalistic system, American democracy are questioned along with everything else from evolutionary theory to Freudian psychology. The interests of this faculty and student body are wide and not narrow. The curriculum is designed to encourage you to learn about a variety of subjects.

If you came to Gustavus to prepare for an occupation and train for a profession, you will get what you came for, but continually you will be challenged to widen your interests, and exchange them for larger ones. You will be given assignments and take courses that have no direct and practical value for professional skill in your field. Gustavus wants you to become better human beings, persons with wide interests, liberal sympathies and rich imaginations. Not only in courses, but at concerts, public lectures, plays, and dormitory conversations your mind will be liberated from the narrowness and conservatism of your childhood so that you can graduate a more mature and sensitive human being.

Do not betray the liberal arts tradition while you are here. Be sure that you deliver it to successive classes and exemplify it wherever you go.

The Tradition of Education in the Context of the Christian Faith

Gustavus is not just a college of scholars associated together in keeping the liberal arts tradition of pursuit of truth and nurture of curiosity alive. It is a Christian college. The tradition that most deeply shapes and informs its entire history and program is the Christian tradition. This tradition is not primarily a set of doctrines or values to believe or a code of rules to obey. It is a meaningful history. The Church is the community of believers who communicate from generation to generation what God has done. Christian education seeks to implant into the natural life stream of every person the redemptive history of God's revelation. This tradition gives a person a history that becomes the continuity and context of his personal life. It gives a person a past and a future. It points to the mystery of his origin and the mystery of his destination.

Gustavus has an important part to play in helping you to make your Christian heritage meaningful in terms of your growing knowledge of the world and yourself. This tradition means that we are committed to conducting ourselves as scholars within the context of God's mercy, to treating one another as persons with love, sympathy and patience. This tradition commits us to a respect for sound scholarship, a passion for knowing about all that God has created, a profound respect for the gifts of language and intellect, and an interest in all events in terms of their relation to God's purposes.

One of the visible ways of being true to this tradition is placing the study of religion at the center of the curriculum. We are moved by our commitment to Jesus Christ to regard the truth of God to be as essential as the truth about man and nature. God's claim on us is unconditional and awakens in us the obligation to bring all of our expanding knowledge into a meaningful relationship with our faith in Christ. Gustavus has a deep ambition to help you develop a mature faith, capable of being expressed in more critical judgments and deeper loyalties. It is as essential for you to go beyond an elementary knowledge of religion as it is to go beyond that level of knowledge to other subjects.

Courses in religion require the same degree of academic discipline and achievement as other courses. You have to pass, and it is possible to get As. But your personal faith is not graded. You are free to hold whatever convictions you choose. You will be challenged, shaken, confused, stretched, and enlightened by new insights in the area of religion. You will have to demonstrate that you have a grasp of new ideas. But you are free to arrive at your conclusion about religious faith. As long as you do good work you will get good grades, even if you are an atheist. If you do not do good work you will get poor grades even if you went to church camp for four years and have taught Sunday School since the ninth grade.

One of the most cherished traditions at Gustavus is the open mind and academic freedom in the study of religion. If you are a person who is not afraid to think, to ask questions, to challenge inherited beliefs, you will be true to this tradition. If you came here to protect your inherited faith from the winds of modern thought you will betray this tradition.

Another tradition which is in keeping with our Christian commitment is daily chapel from 10 to 10:20 a.m. Since this practice of daily chapel is so unusual and strange in the pattern of modern life, you may wonder why it is so important here.

And it is important--so important that it was once required that students attend every day. You will be freed from all other appointments during that 20 minutes. No one has the authority to detain you to finish some work. Buildings normally accessible will be closed to you during chapel. It may take you four years of attending chapel before you begin to realize the importance and what an influence it had on your life. Only after graduation will you really feel its full impact.

By this act God is exalted in your life. You are reminded that you are responsible to Him. Your vision of life's purpose will be brought back into focus. Your heart will be refreshed by adoration of God. Your sense of what is valuable and important in life will be sharpened. Your conscience will be rebuked by God's judgment. The vital center of your selfhood will be assaulted by the power of God's Word as Christ is raised anew in you, cleansing you by forgiveness and enlivening you with love. The benefits are intangible and long term. To deprive your spirit of them is like depriving your body of nourishing food and refreshing air.

It will require a good measure of self-discipline on your part to attend daily--a measure that very few of you will have if one can go by the record of the past. Pressures begin to pile up. The example of those who betray this tradition by going in other directions at chapel time will be very enticing. I can only urge you to preserve this empty place in the daily schedule for worship. If you do not your life will become increasingly harassed and hectic as you try to cover up the embarrassment of having an empty heart that has lost the presence of God.

Gustavus is no sheltered sanctuary of sinless saints. There is a healthy worldliness here and no little opportunity to make your sad mistakes. You will have considerable personal freedom. You will find it just as easy to be a sinner here as anywhere else. You will be tempted to do wrong, not by your enemies but by your friends. You will find that the popular alternative at Gustavus is not always the right one. You will find academic sloth, profanity, vulgarity, cattiness, disregard of property, snobbishness, idle complacency, boredom and the priggishness of self-styled saints.

But because Gustavus is a Christian college it stands under the judgment of God and is a place where we all are made aware of the perversion of personality and the corruption of community which sin breeds.

Tradition and You

The real question is will you inherit and deliver the Gustavus traditions or betray them? To make the grade as a Gustie is more than being an expert at having a good time, more than being elected to the Guild of St. Ansgar, more than being a top student, or a star athlete---although it can be all of these. More than these is being a Christian student, whose knowledge is tempered by humility, whose skill is inspired by love, whose courage is linked to faith and whose realism is cleansed and uplifted by hope.

Gustavus, The Church and the Changing Tradition

DJ: When Esbj arrived as a faculty member at Gustavus, the College was unambiguous about its Christian goals and objectives. From the catalog (1952-54):

Believing that the fundamental purpose of Christian education is to develop Christian personality and to prepare the student for creative living and effective service to church and society, Gustavus Adolphus College commits itself to the following aims and objectives. To impart knowledge of the background, faith and ideals of Christianity to all its students, to encourage their personal commitment to Christ as the Saviour and to Christianity as the Way of Life; and to hold before them at all times the conviction that every vocation is a Divine calling.

To accomplish those goals and objectives, the College chiefly hired faculty and staff who shared those aims and objectives. The College required every student to take a course within the Christianity Department for every semester in residence at the College except for one semester in the senior year. Further, daily chapel attendance was required and the roll was taken. Persons with an excessive number of chapel cuts were invited to a conversation with the president.

Today's prospective student and prospective faculty member would hardly recognize the aims and objectives of the 1952 catalog and the requirements imposed. Students today are required to take one course in religion (substantially within the Christian tradition); and chapel has not been required since 1962. While Gustavus has remained faithful to its mission, it hardly needs to be stated that the college has dramatically changed in the past 50 years in the way it both states that mission and the ways in which it is lived out. In hindsight, the changes are dramatic, but the College has evolved slowly to its present position.

A college is always in a process of change. Students graduate, new students arrive. Faculty leave or retire and are replaced by new faculty. Presidents retire and new leadership comes. Boards are limited to terms to be replaced by new members. Change is natural. Change also comes as institutions engage in long-range planning and intentionally plan to respond to new opportunities, needs, and challenges.

The process of more dynamic and far-reaching changes was set in motion by President Carlson and the board of trustees who, as the College approached its centennial year in 1962, established a Long Range Planning Committee. Esbjornson was part of the curriculum committee. In a talk to the alumni of the college, Esbj outlined and summarized the College's evolutionary development, especially with respect to the study of religion.

From a Christianity Department to a Religion Department

RE: In 1962, the name of the department was changed from the Christianity Department to the Department of Religion. The graduation requirement was changed from one two-credit course every semester to three basic courses, Bible, Church History and either Christian Doctrine or Christian Ethics. This was all part of the curricular reform of 1962.

In 1962, Christ Chapel was built and, in keeping with the times and best worship practices, chapel was no longer compulsory.

In 1968, there was a further reduction to two courses in religion, "substantially in the Christian tradition." In1972, the only requirement was one course in religion, again, "substantially in the Christian tradition." A second course in religion could fulfill a humanities requirement, and a course in World Religions could fulfill the non-Western studies requirement established in the 1962 reform." One of the consequences of this change is that only about one third of the students have a course in Bible. Two alternatives could be chosen, a Studies in Religion course, or a Religion in America course. In the late 1980s, the structure of the department offerings was reorganized under four headings: Bible, Christian Thought, Religion and Culture, and History of Religions or World Religions

DJ: Esbjornson would later refer to the reduction in requirements as a disaster for the serious study of faith and the Christian tradition. *Letter to Dr.Ted Conrad, 1987.*

Esbjornson participated in the decisions for the changes. In 1972, he reluctantly read the "handwriting on the wall" and chose to look at the positive aspects of the further reduction in requirements. Esbj believed that it was now the obligation, opportunity and challenge for the religion department faculty to make courses so interesting and relevant that students would choose to take courses in the department rather than be forced by requirements into the study. Esbj put his imagination and creativity to work. That story is recorded in a subsequent chapter on Esbj as Teacher and Mentor.

Changes in Faculty make-up

RE: Before 1962 all faculty members in the Christianity department were male, Lutheran and ordained clergy. A decision to diversify and strengthen the academic qualifications of the whole faculty was the result of a series of seminars in which college personnel and clergy from the Minnesota Conference (synod) participated. The clergy, from the supporting congregations, by a significant majority, endorsed the emphasis on diversity and quality, even if it meant choosing people who were not affiliated with the Lutheran Church. The result was that about twice as many non-Lutherans joined the faculty in the years from 1960-1970.

Esbj on Diversity

RE: Our world is very much in need of what Jesus personified in his ministry (e.g. reaching out to the outcasts, to minorities and to women). In a pluralistic society, not exclusiveness and prejudice but inclusiveness and hospitality to others different from us are very essential. Diversity is not going to disappear. As knowledge expands, so does variety. From Jesus we learn to be true to ourselves and hospitable to others. *Scandia Grove Lutheran Church sermon, 1982*

Hospitality

DJ: Again, in response to this emphasis on diversity, Esbj led the way in welcoming newcomers into the community. He and Ruth did this personally by opening their home to new faculty members, by offering friendship and encouragement. Esbj in a chapel talk in 1996, recounted the hospitality he was afforded as an outsider by the Benedictines of St. John's Abbey while he was on sabbatical. He spoke of the Gustavus tradition of welcoming which he insisted was a direct expression of its Lutheran character.

RE: Gustavus welcomed scholars from a variety of other traditions. They came: the Sudermans, Koehler, Masons, Owens, Fullers, Brews, Prehns, Govers, Deans, Hyers, Ludwigs, Freierts, Buechmanns, Rezmerskis, and others. They have given color and character to Gustavus, which without them would have been duller and perhaps dead by now. I am glad for them. I hope they have felt the friendliness of Gustavus. *Faculty Notes*, No. 3, 1995/96

Esbj's Angst

DJ: A lover with such enthusiasm for the ideals and possibilities of the Christian College and who felt so blessed by that kind of education could only feel conflicted as changes continued. Esbj lamented that few faculty joined in daily chapel. He lamented every sign of loss of community and of higher and higher standards of excellence while qualities of justice, compassion and community took a back seat. He lamented the change in terminology for this type of school- - from Christian college, to church college to church-related college.

In the late '80s, Esbj joined Bernhard Erling and others in a failed attempt to increase the religion requirements to two courses. The second course, supported by Dean David Johnson, would have been a senior capstone course in ethics and values. Even as Gustavus was moving away from required religion courses, it was increasing its concern for issues of peace, justice and social concerns. In the '60s, a Peace Studies Program was added under the leadership of Bernard Layfatte, Jr., a protégé of Martin Luther King, Jr. An annual MayDay Conference was started in 1981, underwritten by Gustavus benefactors Florence and Raymond Sponberg. It originally focused on the nuclear threat and since has taken on a variety of topics dealing with threats to world peace. The Sponbergs also established a Chair in Ethics which has rotated among professors from several different departments. A new Environmental studies program at Gustavus is now in place capitalizing on students' interest in the environmental movement. A theologian/ethicist has been part of nearly every Nobel Conference. Issues of peace and justice show up regularly in a variety of courses. First Term Seminar courses are designed to address questions of values and are offered across every department. Regular conferences address racism, economic disparity, hunger, war and gender and sexuality issues. Concern for ethics has moved across the curriculum.

Esbj applauded each of these developments and contributed during his time. However, he cautioned that ethics should not be cut off from the firm grounding in the Christian tradition and its understanding of the love of God and humanity. His own study of history made him dubious.

RE: It gives pause for speculations about the future. Will GAC go the way of so many other colleges founded by churches--colleges of high quality liberal arts education with a minimal attention to what was once important in colleges of the Church? We seem to be well on the way along a path well-trodden in American educational history. Is the momentum so powerful that nothing can be done to stop it--given the cultural diversity of our society, our faculty and, increasingly, our students?

If any trend is observable at Gustavus it is the lessening emphasis on this responsibility for transmitting the Christian faith and the gradual reduction of opportunities in the curriculum for students to be engaged in that task. 1995

DJ: Bill Dean, Esbj's longtime colleague in the Department of Religion, contributed a great deal to the growing secularization of Gustavus. When Esbjornson and Erling were working to increase the religion requirements, Dean opposed such a move. He often disagreed with Esbjornson although each had great respect for the other. Dean thought Esbj's writings on the traditions and character of Gustavus said more about "the heart of Esbj" than it did about the college (letter from Dean to Esbjornson, 1987). When Dean received an invitation to join the faculty at Iliff School of Theology in Denver, he penned some "farewell thoughts" for *Faculty Notes*. Dean understood the value of the Gustavus tradition, even as he pushed the college in new directions. He wrote:

Finally, and most significantly, I am leaving a college in the midst of a significant evolution. To describe this evolution isn't easy. It seems to have something to do with a move from a regional, denominational, communal college to a more national college with binocular vision: one eye on the student, the other on worlds of scholarship and culture. Two good administrations have nurtured this evolution. An increasingly heterogeneous and prestigious faculty has given it the necessary intellectual leadership. But the college has not yet decided whether or how to combine its new professionalism with its old moral, spiritual, and communal sensibility. After my years at Gustavus and after looking at schools quite unlike Gustavus, I can see the importance of letting neither aspect prevail. The school that combines them will set a new standard, particularly if it keeps the larger world in mind. Faculty Notes, 1995/96, No. 3

This was Dean's hope--as well as Esbjornson's

Robert Esbjornson, S.T.M.
Associate Professor of Christianity
and Head of Department
Gustavian, 1960

Chapter Five:

Esbj as Teacher and Mentor

DJ: Many Gustavus students and staff claim Esbj as mentor. I am also one of those claimants. Mentoring, we have come to realize, is one of the main roles of a professor at a liberal arts college, especially a church-related, liberal arts college. Gustavus, today, places a premium on the mentoring that faculty and other staff offer. Esbj, in a sermon preached on the occasion of the installation of Diane Havlik Shallue '71 as an Associate in Ministry, offered this observation about being a mentor:

RE: Diane calls me her mentor, but I disclaim that. At best I am like a midwife with some knowledge of pregnancy and birthing, who can be helpful at times of need; but no one can bear or give birth to a child for another. I could listen, encourage and occasionally reassure Diane, but only she could go through those deaths and resurrections that mark the story of maturing faith.

DJ: In 1983, Gustavus was invited to nominate two faculty persons to be considered for the CASE (Council for the Advancement of Secondary Education) "Teacher of the Year" Award. Gustavus brought forth the names of Richard Fuller (physics) and Bob Esjbornson (religion). The college solicited letters of recommendation from faculty and former students. Their nominating letters capture what it was about Esbj that so impacted their lives. Here are some quotes from the letters:

"Esbj's guidelines kept returning to me, months and years after the course had ended and I grappled with life's ethical problems........There has never been another teacher like him. Esbj meets the world with an eclectic mind. He reads widely--traditional writings and radical ones. His synthesized ideas are by turn playful and creative, sober and reflective. He is fresh and never trite and he shows a clarity of vision altogether too rare, even among academics. The man is exceptional. In my ten years of undergraduate and graduate training, there has never been another teacher like him." **Susan Busch Leaf '71**

"Esbj has been permanently etched in my memory as so full of vitality and life that it is impossible to walk away the same person after an encounter with him." **Jana Luipakka** (student at the time of the nomination).

"Bob Esbjornson continues to be for me an artist of sorts; a spinner of connections, an explorer of interdisciplinary linkages. Simplistic associations of sacred

55

and secular hold few boundaries for him. ....I experienced him as an innovator, demanding, competent, yet particularly caring and empathetic. ....For many of us he was the guide, the first explorer into the deepest mysteries of ethics, literature, history. A kind of companion of the heart, he continues to remain for me a philosophical guide, teacher and fellow traveler." **Jon Magnuson '67.**

"You worked hard at getting us to comprehend a basic and thorough introduction to the rudiments of the classic Christian faith. It was there in a remarkable way in the patient teaching that you did. But the most important thing you imparted was the excitement and clear inspiration that faith brought to your own life, which we could see for ourselves was there. It was an obvious reality for you, and that was the priceless gift you shared.

It would take at least an entire book to describe what you mean to me--to explicate how you have taught me to think and to pray and to analyze ethical situations, to see the beauty of daffodils and ocean waves, to experience awe and wonder in worship, to know grace, and, most importantly, to know God in a consequential way. I first knew you as a committed and amazing teacher, then as a sensitive homilist and worship leader, then as my adviser and counselor, then as a boss, then as a loyal supporter during my seminary years, then as my ordination sponsor--and now and always as my spiritual father, mentor and cherished friend. I would not be who I am had it not been for you. Your exuberant joy in life, your profound faith in God, your radical yet gentle commitment to peace and to the stewardship of the earth, your incredible creativity in thinking and writing, your solid and yet innovative teaching, your letters and poetry, and your belief in me even when I have doubted myself--all of this is of pervading and indelible importance to me." **S. Anita Stauffer '69**

"Professor Esbjornson's teaching serves as a model against which we now measure our own instructional philosophy and practice. More than any other teacher we have known, he continually searches for and employs ever more effective ways of involving his students in meaningful inquiry." **David '69 and Jane Norman Leitzman '69**

"More than anyone else, Professor Esbjornson has proved to me that the spirit of youth may linger long and that aging can be an exciting and creative process." **Sue Williams, 83**

"It is now almost 30 years since we left his classroom, but the impact of his teaching and his personal example continues strongly to the present time. Indeed, the force of his talents and personality have taken on legendary proportions, not only to us, but to the greater Gustavus community at large. He stands as a shining example of total dedication and immersion in liberal arts education.

56

We have never encountered a teacher with such intense enthusiasm for his work and this has not diminished in the slightest degree over the years." **Richard '55 and Lucille Fogelstrom DeRemee '56**

"I cite him as one of the most insightful, scholarly, and innovative educators that I have ever known. He, perhaps more than any other, was singularly responsible for my career in clinical and academic medicine. (His)…vision and breadth of knowledge not only encompasses the esoteric, but also the realm of scientific and medical research, political reality, ethics and solid social systems. His teaching style is fluid; his humanity befriends his students. His gifts to students are imparted by vehicles of lectures, sermon, song, dance, scenario, books, poems, and encounters." **Mark E. Clasen '69**

Esbj's Ecocratic Man

DJ: In this highly edited 1970 sermon preached at Good Shepherd Lutheran Church in Duluth, Minnesota, Esbj spoke plainly about the student revolt taking place on campuses everywhere. Esbj reveals his unique way of approaching these students: with love, understanding and a desire to learn from them. Esbj had hope for what they could bring and also feared that they might crash on their own excesses. It is both a look at the times and a look at the caring professor who grounded his hope not in the students themselves, but in the God of history.

RE: At Gustavus we have all of the manifestations of the youth culture, in moderation, but nonetheless real: Long hair and loud music and colorful, shabby clothes; the drug cult, Women's Liberation Movement, Black Power, War Protest, Save --the --Environment campaign. Buttons reading "Make love, not war." Students' Rights movement, asking for more self-determination in dormitory living and more voice in policymaking.

Two episodes on May 1 (May Day) illustrate my observations. In my freshman religion class on Fridays students are given a chance to teach me and one another about what they have learned and how they feel about some phase of religion. On May 1, a group of students performed a parody of the Lutheran liturgy. The "minister" wore a two-faced mask. The scripture lessons were fragmentary and meaningless short excerpts taken out of context. The sermon was about the need for the purchase of a snowmobile so that the minister could do "missionary" work among the Indians of Sugar Hill (a winter ski resort). In the discussion afterwards several students agreed that, though exaggerated, the parody expressed how they felt about services in their home congregations and at college. They claimed that they felt more religious at a recent John Denver Concert than at services in Christ Chapel. These students are some of the best I have, not a core of radicals.

The second episode took place at Convocation in the chapel while the college was observing Law Day by hearing District Judge Noah Rosenblum speak about the judiciary system. Shortly after his speech began, four students carried a black student tied to a chair and gagged. They placed him on the chancel platform near the pulpit; a black-robed black student stood by him. After a brief exchange between the students and the convocation chairman about giving the speaker the freedom to speak, the judge continued and completed his speech without interruption. But the tableaux beside him made us all keenly aware that the political, legal and police system does not guarantee justice for the black man in our society because that society itself has and still does tolerate the belief that the white man is inherently superior to the black man. This episode was planned and executed by a black student who is one of the more creative thinkers enrolled in my religion classes, not a "bum" which is the label President Nixon used for protesting students.

At Gustavus we are confronted with and perplexed by the student revolt against the institutions and ideas we have respected and cherished. There are those who would like to blame it on the radical professors they have, but that explanation will not do. Students are in revolt against their professors, too. And they are already in revolt when they come to college.

I turn to a woman, one of the world's greatest, for a clue to help explain what is going on. Margaret Mead, in an article called "Youth Revolt: The Future is Now," offers an explanation that makes considerable sense. She says, *We are entering a totally new phase of cultural evolution, and all persons born before 1945 are immigrants in a new age, just as our forbears were immigrants in a new land. The new generation, the articulate rebels around the world who are lashing out against the controls imposed on them, are like the first generation born in this country. They are natives at home in this time. Satellites are familiar to their skies…They have never known a time when war did not threaten their annihilation.…When given the facts, they can understand immediately that continued pollution will make the planet uninhabitable. As members of an expanding world population and of one world species they recognize that distinctions of race and caste are no longer valid…In their eyes killing an enemy is not qualitatively different from murdering a neighbor. They cannot escape a system that indiscriminately destroys other's children with napalm and uses every means to save and make comfortable our own children.…*

They not only know these things,.…they feel them, which it is difficult for their elders to do because their feelings were conditioned by the experience of an earlier age.…

In this situation parents and teachers are no longer guides. There are no guides who understand the future which our generation created but cannot control. Youth are looking for and shaping new ways of thinking, feeling, and doing that will enable them to cope with a new era in man's long evolution. I have a course in Christian ethics which focuses upon the future and the problems which this new generation will have to solve if mankind is to make it into its next phase of development. As the semester progressed the class acted more and more strangely: there was little discussion; the students were silent and subdued, even sullen and hostile. One day I could stand it no longer and rebelled against teaching until I found an explanation. I discovered that they felt overwhelmed by the future with which they would have to cope. Instead of being near to stoning me they were stoned by future shock and they found my presentation of Christian ethics quite unconvincing. I, too, am struggling to find ways of coping with this new age. I realize I am an immigrant and my students are natives of this time.

It is in this cultural context that I want to place the future of the church college, Gustavus in particular. I would put it this way: It cannot be, in the words of our alma mater, "Gustavus Adolphus, remember thy past" and try to impose it upon the new generation. If we attempt to preserve old moralities and institutional practices and pieties, the College will pass from the scene or be abandoned by the Church. Nor is its mission: "Right on, Gustavus, right on." We can't just "go with the students and bless their bulldozers and their pots of acid and make their slogans the new ideology.

The mission of Gustavus is to give courage to youth so that they will not be afraid of the future they must face and cannot escape. This is what the elders can best give them, even if they can give them no certain answers. It may surprise them to find in that ancient book, the Bible, the images of the godly revolution we are looking for. Moses led the people out of the oppression of the Egyptian system into the wilderness where they had to struggle for survival. The bread of freedom was manna, there today and gone tomorrow. But they had the promise of God that he would give them a new land and they managed to keep alive, until Moses sent twelve spies into Canaan. As the land of Canaan appeared to Israel, pregnant with promise and full of threat, so the future appears to this generation and its parents. The un-silent majority, now as then, both young and old, is ready to stone the spies who say, "It is a good time in which to live. Let us go forward." They would prefer the flesh pots of the old system of the past than the promise of the future.

Among the educators of youth we need Calebs who say, "This age to come is a challenge!"

"The times ahead are dangerous, but full of promise! "This day, the Lord has made. Let us rejoice and be glad in it."

For the Lord is ahead of us, pulling us and dragging us into future toward the fulfillment of his promise. Jesus himself said to the disciples, "Greater works

59

than these will you do." Moses commissioned Caleb and Joshua to lead the next generation into the land, not the ten cautious spies.

Gustavus aspires to stand in that kind of past--the heritage of futurists who have revolutionized their societies, who have believed in the coming of a new humanity.

Because Gustavus remembers such a past it has a special contribution to make to the new generation. Elders who have seen and survived change--can give faith and hope and love to the young. They have wisdom and perspective to give. The older generation will blow their opportunity if they lose confidence in their offspring and begin to call them bums, effete snobs, and punks.

I want to share my perception of the new kind of man I see emerging amidst the labor pains of these troubled times. Among my generation's children, to whom we have handed an ambiguous legacy of threat and promise, there is being born a new man, *Ecocratic man*.

He is our child, but not our style. He has learned from our compulsive productivity the necessity of play and celebration. He will have his Woodstock Nation, where the price of admission is $1, but if you don't have the buck, come in just the same. He feels that the whole world should be made successful for everybody, not just whites, not just American, not just allies. He believes the Earth's resources belong to us all and he resents the exploiter who thinks he owns the air and river as his private sewer. He cannot accept old claims for private gain, the public be damned; let the consumer beware. He would delight in both trees and buildings, cats and computers, he would be fascinated by the intricate workings of a technocratic society and also by the complex web of life in a forest. He would manage, not maul, the land.

He would heed the protests of the poor against a system that awards fat research grants and academic freedom to scientists and penalizes welfare mothers with demeaning morality checks and snoopers peering under beds for hidden lovers. He would value supremely not affluence, but wholeness. He would be a citizen of the whole world, and be tender toward all living things. He would see himself not as alien to and above nature but in it and responsive to it and responsible for what he does in it.

Ecocratic man is pressing against the pelvic bones, straining to be born. His birth among us, among our youth, fills father with troubled dreams and mother with pain. But his coming is as irresistible as the birth of a baby. He is bone of our bone, blood of our blood. His symbolic heritage goes back to the first faint glimmerings in man's imagination of what he might someday become. Ecocratic man's coming is not a dream; it is an event. It is the future rushing toward us, so strange, and yet not so strange. We fear him, and we love him. Ecocratic man comes, but not without all the risks of being human.

He is tempted by pride, as were his forbears from the beginning. He is tempted to destroy, under the rubric of revolution. He is tempted to neglect the disciplines of hard thought that his complicated world requires of him. He would celebrate, when he has nothing to show for all his highs. He would thumb his nose at God, as if in his strength he found safety.

He would dissolve mystery in pots of acid, and blow from his mind reverence for the One in whom he lives and moves and has his being.

I teach at a college I care about. How I hope for Gustavus to be a college for the next generation! A college for ecocratic man, a college where hopes are fired by vision.

A college that is not afraid to be ahead of the Church, and a Church that is no longer afraid to be a pilgrim commune, leading and pulling us all into the future which we both fear and desire. I say to my fellow teachers in our clumsy way, let's try to learn from as well as teach, our students. And if we cannot change our deeply embedded habits, let us at least convey hope and not disillusionment, faith and not scorn and mistrust, love and not divisiveness and derision.

And to you, Christ, man of the future, reborn in us each day, sustain us by your cosmopolitan grace and encourage us when we falter.

Esbj: A Creative Teacher in a Creative College

DJ: Esbj could not have become the teacher he was without a college that was daring enough to encourage creativity in teaching. The College was, and is, committed to innovation and change. Esbj personally credits Dean Albert Swanson for supporting his ideas for innovation in the classroom. The curriculum reforms of 1962 and the early '70s involved significant changes. The Nobel Conference, inaugurated in 1965, encouraged all faculty and students to be engaged with the theme for the year. Writing across the curriculum drew the attention of academic journals across the country. Gustavus was an early leader in establishing a 4-1-4 academic year which permitted the rise of January term courses. Professors used this time most creatively. The Edgar M. Carlson Award, in the first years, was for "Innovative Teaching." Today it is for "Distinguished Teaching." The original title indicates the premium the College was placing on innovation.

Esbj responded--creatively. He developed an Urban Church January Term in cooperation with the Ecumenical Institute (traveling to Chicago) and later, following the changing concerns of students, a study course on prayer and spiritual life. But the changes were not in just *what* he taught, but the *way* he taught.

RE: In the 1950s I learned that my course and I were not the most important affairs in students' lives. My image of the relationship with students and colleagues changed from the picture of a prof in front of a class on an elevated platform facing students sitting in rows of chairs. The only significant relation-ship was between me and each student individually. Do you remember sitting in crowded rows facing the professor? Did it unconsciously cause you to address every remark to him and to no one else? I saw that happen again and again. Later, I saw a different image, a sphere of circular balls with lines connecting everybody, not just lines to me. This image was suggested by models of the mol-ecule.　　　*Presentation in 2000 to the class of 1955.*

DJ: With the reduction of a religion requirement to one semester, Esbj dis-continued teaching the Bible as the single focus. To teach the Bible in a single semester was an impossible task, he reasoned. It was better to teach portions of the Bible to give students a method of approaching the entire Bible. He also felt that skeptical students would be more open to a study of religion. Thus, he developed a phenomenological approach.

RE: I decided in the early '70s to teach a Studies in Religion course rather than Bible. The content was substantially Biblical and about Christian com-munities. What appeared in this new way of teaching? What was out there in that vast field? Not something new but something I had scarcely noticed. The empirical data was phenomena common to a wide range of communities, vivid religious experiences, stories and testimonies, rituals, beliefs, and moral rules. Theologians and Biblical scholars were not the only scholars interested in reli-gion. So were psychologists, sociologists, philosophers, historians, semiologists, even futurologists, each with their own perspectives and concerns. There were three basic questions among these scholars. One was the origin, development, and the changes and continuities in religious life--the temporal perspective. A second concerned the functions of religion in personal development and in so-cial groups--the concerns of psychologists and sociologists. And, the third, the meaning of religions--both the rational and the expressive aspects in beliefs and in the arts of religion.

I developed a model for my students that included all these perspectives. This was the scholar's way of seeking an understanding of religion.

Diggametrip

DJ: Thus, Esbj developed *Digametrip* as a way of enticing students into this new way of looking at the study of religion. *Digametrip* was a combination of Dig, Game and Trip

Esbj frequently used James Michener's *The Source* in his Bible courses. It was very popular with students. It gave them an in-depth and continuous story about Biblical times and beyond. But the book also gave Esbj a new metaphor for history. His spatial image of history had been a horizontal line from past to present. The tell gave him an image of layers piled on top of each other, a per-pendicular image.

RE: I was using phenomenology to teach religion and Bible. It comes from the Greek word, *to appear.* It is the study of that which displays itself. But it is more than just an observation, it is an *entering into.* Digging into someone is trying to see, to understand, to accept someone as he or she is, and not make judgments about that someone.

To explain this teaching concept, I wrote essays on each aspect. Often I put them in the form of conversations with students. I knew the students' concern about studying religion and tried to draw them in with imaginative and playful essays.

One of my imaginary student asks, "You mean that 'the dig' is an image you use for the investigation of both personal religion and the religions of societies---people's religions, don't you?" "Correct." I explained further. The dig keeps us thinking in terms of depth--historical depths of religious tradition and the psychological depths of personal experience. The digs were down into the collective unconscious, wherein lies the origin of all the primitive instincts of religion.

What lies beyond myths, rituals, beliefs and practices? What are the ancient truths that cannot be discarded or ignored and that are part of life today whether we acknowledge them or not? It is, not a study of the peripheral in life, but the most important, exciting, adventurous journey in life. It is the discovery of the Self, not in isolation, but in relationships to the family, the tribe, the nation and the world.

I couldn't help but ask the student, "Can you dig it?"

Game

RE: One of my discoveries during teaching the studies course was that art forms were far more prevalent and significant than I had realized. My training, conventional in the guild of Euro-American scholarship, was strong on literary, historical and theological criticism. I learned to deal with written texts and to participate in intellectual conversations. The arts express more than they explain. Symbols are dense, complex, multivalent, expressing more than one message in a single symbol. The arts allow for the wisdom of emotions and supplement the wisdom of reason. I introduced a unit in the course about ritual in the life story, the connections between change, moral choices and ritual celebrations. This was to become a key component of the new phenomenological approach.

In these imaginary conversation with students, one of them says, "My religion is personal, my own. I have a strong feeling about it and am afraid to expose it to you or anyone. I am not sure I want to study it or dig into it as you say, or share it with others. I may be afraid of what is under the surface, of depths."

She had put her finger on a difficulty that I had wrestled with for a long time in my work as teacher of religion. Religion is a subjective and sensitive affair in the lives of most of us, even those of us who say we are not religious. We are involved as actors, not spectators. Our beliefs, affections, loyalties, life projects and past experiences are affected by any effort to study religion. My dilemma as a teacher is this: we are supposed to be detached, analytical, and academic. How can we maintain such a cool stance when we enter 'the force field' of personal experience and not have a significant and serious effect on people?

My next imaginary friend introduced a problem opposite that of the first and offered, "I'm not a religious person. Religion is old stuff--for grandmas, maybe, but not for my generation. Why do I have to take a religion course?" These two people confronted me with the kind of challenge I often face. One was very religious and the other against religion, and both suspicious about studying religion.

Some students expect devotional and inspirational classes that will nurture their home-based faith. Others fear they will be indoctrinated in beliefs and ideas they do not share. Not so. We do not carry on such classes, not revivals, not catechetical sessions. Even so, the difficulty remains, because when we enter the territory of religion we get into the inner space of personal life and the serious working beliefs of societies. I see no way of avoiding the danger, or the benefit, of affecting people's lives when they engage in the study of religion.

We would not be very smart to ignore religion. To do so results in having an incomplete and distorted view of human culture and experience. Whether you are personally religious or not, you need to understand religion in order to understand others who are and the influences of religion on the society in which you live.

Analysis, comparisons, and all the scholarly methods could have what seem like negative effects. It may be disillusioning at first to discover the social factors that keep certain styles of religion alive, factors that are not directly attributable to "divine presence," and it can be a shock to some people who believe the Bible is the inerrant, infallible Word of God to learn about the historical context of the writings and the variation of literary style and form. But consider this. Dispelling limited notions in order to expand one's knowledge of reality is what education is all about. There are too many illusions about religion. It is better to gain a mature understanding in an academic setting than to go through the trauma of disillusionment later in times of personal crisis. The ultimate aim of the academic study of religion is not destructive but constructive. It is to help people toward a mature and richer understanding that will serve them well during times of personal difficulty when he or she must work through shattering experiences toward mature ways of believing and acting. A person can be religious without having studied religion, just as she can enjoy food without having studied nutrition. In both cases sound knowledge is an asset.

Someone needs to speak up against the cultured despisers of religion in our society, who are so vocal. I only ask students to open up their minds to look at a significant factor in our lives.

The Game is a way to help both the religious and nonreligious student deal with the traps of subjectivity and the fear of analysis. If we study religion as it is, a powerful force in personal life and cultural history, if we expose ourselves to the experiences and traditions of others, we can feel free enough to be open and attentive to and appreciative of what we are studying if we think of it as a game. We can enter the study as we enter a game, in an *as if* frame of mind and *for the time being*. We can play out ideas we do not necessarily have to bring into our daily lives.

But, then, we just might.

The Dromenons or Happenings

RE: I inaugurated a feature called *Dromenons,* from the Greek word for drama. These dramas or happenings were planned and presented by students organized into several small groups or seminars. Their assignment was to study some aspect of religion and then convey what they learned, some idea or theme, by actions and props, not by words or panel discussion. The rest of the class and I were to be involved as participants, not just as spectators passively watching and listening. If you have played charades you have something of an idea of what a Happening is. I was astonished by what developed. Students were creative, imaginative, and playful. We had fun, and we learned something about religion that we could not have gained by just reading and engaging in the usual palaver of classroom talk. The Happenings revealed the artful in religion. In our Western intellectual tradition, especially about religion, we think in the categories of philosophy, history and the written and spoken word. There are aspects of religion that remain obscure and are therefore neglected when we study only by means of words. By using images, artforms, sound, greasepaint, gestures, street theater, masks--we begin to realize that religion has an imaginative, playful and dramatic aspect.

We can try on "other selves," engage in antics, just to learn how they feel to us. We know it is a game in which we are free to think something different from what we believe or know, and to be what we are not yet, or ever, desire to be. In the process of pretending we may actually learn something about being a Sioux or a Muslim that we could learn in no other way.

"I remember with fondness and a chuckle that you used to (literally!) dream up teaching/learning plans in the middle of the night, leaping into the classroom the next day telling us of your 4 a.m. brainstorm on grading or projects or whatever. We often secretly hoped you'd sleep through the night, but then we would marvel at your freshness and enthusiasm that kept us wanting to investigate and study and share with each other our projects." **Nancy Eddy, '66**

"While my teaching lacks the incredible, creative and energetic quality you bring to a classroom, I can say that I have perfected the 'Esbj cluttered desk look,' and I follow the "stash and search" method of filing things. How well I remember those mornings when you would rush down the steps of Uhler Hall, briefcase in hand and hair askew from riding your bike, and you would excitedly tell us about a new idea you had worked out at 4 a.m. With that, you would open your suit jacket, reach into the pocket for your notes, and exclaim, 'Great Scott!! Wrong coat!!'" **Mary J. Trimbo '66**

Trip

RE: I began to use the "Long Search" television series for "trips" into other religions, as well as in Christianity's variations. Those trips were not just touristy affairs for entertainment. I used them to teach students to be observant about religious life and to see common features in a variety of forms. It was a wonderful learning experience meant to enlarge and enrich understanding, not to present other religions as choices to consider.

Trip is an image that points to the beyond, to what is beyond our present and past experience, beyond our own culture, beyond our own times into the future. The study of religion is a trip in that sense.

I first used the word back in the 1960s when the word referred to hallucinatory experiences produced by drugs, such as LSD. There were occasions when the study of religion gave me and students a "high"-- a going beyond ourselves. That is not so strange as ecstasy is an element of religion. Ecstasy: the word means a feeling of overpowering joy, or being beside oneself with feeling. We use the word transcendence (*trans* which in the Latin means "over" and *scandere* for "climb"). We use transcendence to express the experience of going beyond, beyond previous limits, beyond our known capacities.

Trips are risky--as all travel can be. Another Latin word suggests so, the word from which trance comes. Transpire, which means "to die," warns us that when we travel away, when we go into the beyond we die in the sense that the old self and the former knowledge and understanding we had before we took the trip dies. Travel changes you.

The imaginary student asked, "Does that mean that you can't go home again?" I responded, "You can, but you will not see 'home' in quite the same way, and you will be a different person for having taken the trip of exploring religion, just as you would be if you traveled. A change takes place, even though you may not betray or abandon your home town religion."

There was a challenge in it, however. How dare I expose students to other religions which I regarded with deep respect? Maybe these experiences would transport naïve people into enchanting alternatives of their own. We were living in a global society increasingly interactive and multicultural. What would this exposure do to students' inherited beliefs and customs?

The effective strategy came from a Roman Catholic theologian from Notre Dame, John Dunne, in his book, *The Way of all the Earth* which was called "an invitation to cross over to the great Eastern religions--and come back to one's own tradition with new insight." What seems to be occurring is a phenomena we might call "passing over," passing from one culture to another, from one way of life to another, from one religion to another. Passing over is a shifting of standpoint, a going over to the standpoint of another culture, another way of life, and another religion. It is followed by an equal and opposite process we might call "coming back"-- coming back with new insight to one's own culture, one's way of life, one's own religion.

So, what is the role of the teacher? Tour guide? No, that is too protective. I prefer another analogy--the park ranger in a national park. He is hospitable at the visitor center, ready to answer questions. He gives illustrated lectures about features and areas of the park that are not seen by those who only drive through. The lectures are intended to stimulate interest in seeing more of the park and to inspire some to take hikes on the high country trails. He gives instructions, warning and rules for hiking and camping because there are narrow trails along cliff faces, sudden storms in the upper valleys, and grizzly bears that could be dangerous. He may serve as a park policeman who rescues anyone who gets into trouble. My task as a teacher is similar. I point out phenomena of religion that students may either ignore or misunderstand, features that have been in their habitat all along, or variations they may not notice when investigating a strange religion. My challenge is to present religion so attractively that some students at least will be persuaded to go into high country explorations of their own. My responsibility is to give sound instructions about how to make the study worthwhile and to come to the aid of students who get into trouble during the *diggamgetrip*.

The journey away from home and familiar knowledge is a normal process, but not all people move very far. The adventurous explorers seem to be a minority, and this is the case in the area of the study of religion. Most people, it seems to me, do not stray very far from their familiar traditions and practices or for very long. Those who do take the trips Dunne talks about experience a degree of alienation from those who do not do so. The people who do not take the journeys sometimes feel threatened by the ideas and insights of the returned wanderers. Not too many people find other person's travel pictures and stories interesting. So it is that tradition-bound people tend not to be interested in the ideas of people who have been more adventurous. We often experience a conversation being held off from continuing any kind of extended or serious discussion of religion we might like to have. It can be lonely at times. But the journey is worth the price. We often return to our own traditions with new and richer understandings of our own religion and that of others.

DJ: The approach of Dunne, used by Esbj in his own teaching, also characterized Esbj's life as a scholar and as a person. He was eager to roam the world of ideas, "crossing over" to learn, gain insight and then bringing it back to enrich his own tradition and set of beliefs.

Esbj and Interfaith

DJ: In a "World Community Day" chapel talk in November of 1973, Esbj addresses the dilemma for Christians who have a great commitment to Christ but are always very aware of other religions and have serious questions about how to relate to them. The challenge of world religions and our increasing contact with persons of other faiths makes interfaith conversations front and center for a liberal arts college of the Church.

RE: Think of this--and rejoice.

Here in this quiet, remote southern town on the Minnesota River on planet Earth is a tiny international community. It is a colony of the whole planet Earth present in this one place! Represented here on this campus are students from 22 countries. It is a fact, a happening worth celebrating on World Community Day. It gives us a small sign of hope that the centuries-old vision of world brotherhood, of justice and peace, can be experienced even in these troubled and strife-torn times.

Think of this and rejoice twice as happily. In each of the great, living religious traditions gleams the dawn--the light of the vision of the One, God, slow to anger, very loving, universally kind whose tenderness embraces all his creatures. And be glad of heart and free in your minds to believe that sometimes at least we show forth this love in our worship and work.

As I thought about and planned this celebration with the help of the students and others, I came to the "smiling knowledge" of the truth that God has no favorites. Like the jolly stout laughing Buddhas we can all have a big laugh together on ourselves as the "joke" God plays on us. He has played a trick and it turns out to be a treat.

Here we thought from inside our circles that we were God's favorites, when all along God has none. "It is the same justice that comes through faith to everyone" *Romans 3.*

"His mercy is from generation to generation to those who fear him." *The Magnificat*

God opens the paths to universal community, toward the truth that is in Him. As we come close to the One God, we come closer to each other.

I am a Christian. I learned through my forefather's and foremother's faith and in my own faith in Jesus Christ that if I am "in Christ" there is neither Jew

68

nor Greek; neither slave nor free; neither male nor female, for we are all one in Christ! *Galatians 3:27*

It seems quite probable that Paul who wrote those words, would add "neither Christian nor non-Christian." For we have come to times when the word Christian expresses the cultural fact, that the word has a partisan rather than a universal meaning. That would be contrary to Paul's vision of the universality of God he had experienced in Jesus!

All who are one, who in faith trust in God's mercy and love one another as Jesus loved Jew and non-Jew, woman and man, sinner and observer of the law. But which of us, Christian, Jew, Hindu, Moslem, Buddhist, or whoever, can measure, in his own traditions, the magnificence of God? His inexpressible grandeur?

Let us all acknowledge with Richard Niebuhr that "all have a vision of the universal but none has a universal vision." Let us with simple and humble faith admit that, in the word of the hymn:

"the love of God is broader than the measure of men's minds

And the heart of the eternal is most wonderfully kind"   Lutheran Book of Worship, No.290

And love one another and all his creatures as God loves us and all our fellow creatures.

Esbj at St. John's Abbey

Chapter Six

Rooted in Faith: Worship, Prayer and The Word

DJ: It is obvious to the reader how important worship is to the well being of Esbjornson. He never tired of writing about its importance as seen in the essay and sermon included here.

Why I go to chapel
RE: Why have I been coming to chapel day after day for 33 years?

Psalm 84 says it. *How I love your Temple, Lord Almighty.*
How I want to be there.
I long to be in the Lord's Temple
With my whole being I sing for joy to the living God.
How happy are those who live in your Temple,
Always singing praises to You.
How happy are those whose strength comes from You.
Good News Bible

I come to sing praise, not to be praised. I come to receive strength, not to exhibit it.
I come to be made righteous by the grace of Christ, not because I am righteous.
I come because I love the beauty of the House and its music and its people.
I come because I am daily standing in the need of prayer.

I come because I am more than a physical organism, satisfied by food and drink, exercise and rest, more than a social animal needing the attention and affection of others, more than a thinking reed needing to satisfy curiosity and a thirst for knowledge. I am a soul who hungers and thirsts for God.

Psalm 63: *"O God, you are my God, and I long for you.*
My whole being desires you…my soul thirsts for you.
Let me see you in your sanctuary,
Let me see how mighty and glorious you are
Your constant love is better than life itself.

A sign outside of Christ Chapel might say, "Come, all you that hunger and thirst for God, the living God. Welcome!

There is another reason. I come, not just to be comforted and nourished. I come to be challenged. Another word came to me this morning, a word I have heard often here through the years, the word coming through Amos.

> The Lord says, I hate your religious festivals!
> I cannot stand them. Stop your noisy songs.
> I do not want to listen to your harps.
> Instead, let justice flow like a stream
> And righteousness like a river that never runs dry. Amos 5: 21-24

That disturbed my consoling thoughts about worship. Ritual, no matter how faithfully observed, cannot be a substitute for righteousness. Music cannot silence the cry for justice.

Then another ancient one spoke:

> The Lord you are looking for will suddenly come to his temple....
> But who will be able to endure the day when he comes?
> He will come like strong soap, like a fire that refines metal.

Malachi 3, vs 2-3

Next to speak to me was a modern voice, Annie Dillard:

> I do not find Christians...sufficiently sensible of conditions. Does anyone have the foggiest idea of what sort of power we so blithely invoke?Or, as I suspect, does no one believe a word of it? The churches are children playing on the floor with their chemistry sets, mixing up a batch of TNT to kill a Sunday morning. It is madness to wear ladies straw hats and velvet hats to church, we should all be wearing crash helmets...For the sleeping god may wake someday and take offense or the waking god may draw us to where we can never return." Annie Dillard, Teaching a Stone to Talk.

Christ Chapel might be quite a dangerous place. Perhaps there might be a sign outside saying, "Danger. Enter at your own risk" I realize that it is very risky to put one's life into God's life, for God is very much alive. But it is a risk I need, a challenge.

Worship is a subversive activity, stripping me of my rationalizations of my self-interest.

Worship is a dangerous, subversive activity, because it limits the other powers in my life, the false gods and deprives them of their legitimacy. I have a place outside their domination systems where I can take a stand. And it is in this house. Worship is a dangerous and subversive activity, because something may happen to me someday that will change my life, so that I can never be the same.

I never know how the Lord will come. It sometimes comes through the words of a familiar hymn, in the prayer of the day, in the sermon, or in the music. And sometimes in the presence of a person whose constant devotion strengthens mine when I falter. Ours is a smashing God and a saving God. One who is a danger to those who do not yield, a delight to those who do.

Worship and the Holocaust.

DJ: How can God be worshiped after the holocaust and other evil events? In this sermon preached in the Presbyterian Church of Kasota in July of 1984, Esbj lays out the case for worship as essential for the well-being of the world.

Text: "Do not fear those who can kill the body....." *Matthew 10:28*

RE: One of the haunting questions that has disturbed people profoundly shaken by the holocausts of the 20th century is the question about God.

Is it possible to believe in, trust, and fear God after one has been appalled and profoundly hurt by the experience of seeing the cruel killing of millions by tyrants and terrorists, by those in government and their opponents who use physical and psychological violence to subdue others.

Where is God when people cry out to him for help and protection from those who are hurting them? We may not be directly threatened by tyrants, not as yet. Terrorists are still a rarity in our society, but they could strike at anytime or place. We are more apt to be hurt by the outbreak of family violence, for most killings by murder are family related.

And we know we have the most to fear from careless and drunken drivers on the road.

There is in all of us a latent fear of those who can kill the body and there is a rational basis for much fear. To be physically destroyed is to be deprived of earthly existence, and we cherish deeply the goodness of life. To be physically abused is to be told you are of no value to the abuser. You annoy me, get out of my way. To be told one is of no value by others, by government or neighbor or family is a profoundly hurtful blow to one's capacity to live.

I repeat my question. Can we believe in, fear, love and trust God and want to worship him after we have seen and experienced the public and personal holocausts of our age?

Imagine yourself in the last moment of life as a murderer begins to abuse you, hurt you and is about to kill you. Your last experience of life is that of terror and that horrible, mad, angry killer's face.

Violent actions of humans against other humans are the most disturbing and most destructive experiences we know. They are attacks on what we value most, our own lives, our trust in other people and our faith in God.

Yet, I dare to say, YES, we can believe in, fear, trust and love God and worship him--even after being profoundly disturbed and shaken by confronting the holocausts of history and realizing they could happen again and could happen to us.

We not only can imagine doing so, we will do so. So do survivors who have had such experiences. Elie Wiesel, famed Jewish novelist who survived the Nazi Holocaust, tells a story which took place in one of the concentration camps.

73

Some of the Jews decided to hold a trial in which God was accused of crimes against humanity. One rabbi was defense counsel. Another was the prosecutor. Others served as jurists. After several days of testimony, the jury found God "guilty." Then one of the rabbis said, "Come, let us go to our prayers."

Yes, people who have been tortured and survived still worship. Yes, families who have lost a dear one to violent killers or careless drunken drivers still go to church to worship. Yes, you and I do. We are here, even though we have lived in this cruel and violent century, even though our own lives are in daily danger from the random violence and the threat of nuclear war. We do believe, we do fear, love and trust God.

This is a mystery, isn't it? There is something very, very deep going on in your heart right now. Ask yourself the question why, why you continue to worship, come here Sunday after Sunday, to pray, to attend to God's word, to honor God. How is it that we can still pray knowing that praying will not ultimately protect us, not one of us from dying, or suffering?

Ludwig Feuerbach, in the 19th century, thought hard about this. He came to the conclusion that many have accepted. Our belief in God, reasoned Feuerbach, is just a projection of wishful thinking, a psychological invention to comfort us in times of our troubles. There is no real God. What we worship is an illusion. Feuerbach laid the foundation for modern atheism and it has been the argument that influenced both Marx and Freud.

But, are we so sure Feuerbach was right? Is not his argument itself a dogmatic assertion with little evidence? Is it not based on a particular and false concept of god, at least false to the most profound experiences incorporated in the traditions of mature religions?

Jesus knew violence in his society. There were terrorists and tyrants. In his boyhood years there was a revolt of patriotic Jews against the Roman government. It was crushed and several thousand Jews were crucified in Galilee. Yet it was Jesus who said, "Fear not those who kill the body, but cannot kill the soul. Rather fear him who can cast both body and soul into hell."

Jesus' life ended in torture and cruel death, apparently defeated. It was Jesus who said, "Fear not, you are of more value than the sparrows." It was Jesus who taught us to understand that if we honor him, the One who affirms our value, who shows mercy, he will honor us before his Father in heaven.

Our value is not destroyed by terrorists or tyrants. It is not insured by either our goodness or our capacity for fear and loyalty in the face of cruelty and pain to ourselves and others.

It is given to us. God values us. Once we believe that, we value ourselves and others, too. It is that inner sense of value rising up from our very bones, our deepest feelings that keep us caring for and about life, wanting to live and let live.

It is this, I believe, that awakens us to the impulse to pray and worship. There is a sense in us of something heavenly, eternal and good. It keeps the human race going in spite of all our defeats and pain.

Why do we gather together for prayer and worship? Because we need each other's encouragement as the sense of our value is vulnerable to the blows to self-respect and love of life. We are, all of us, quite capable of sliding into disrespect of others and despising ourselves.

We need to hear one another's stories and see one another here. Think of how encouraging it is to us to see at worship someone who has suffered an awful blow, someone who can say with Job, even with tears in his eyes "though God slay me, yet will I trust him."

There is also an important public reason for worship here, together. It has been very much on my mind this last week because of a conversation with Father Michael of St. John's Abbey about an article written by ethicist John Pawlikowski in the latest issue of "Worship" periodical. Father Michael summarized it for me in these words:

Nazism arose in Germany, a nation with a high level of education and culture. But science, technology, the arts, philosophy, not even ethics and theology could prevent the holocaust. The universities yielded to Hitler, the churches were used by Hitler. There were a few voices of protest, including those of pastors and theologians but they were not strong enough to prevent the holocaust.

What happened in Germany was the decline of worship, the decrease in participation, the diminishment of the community of the faithful. There was not corporate encouragement of this sense of value of persons. The result was the slaughter of Jews and others, not just by the consequences of war but a deliberate bureaucratic government sponsored, efficiently organized, technologically competent program of killing. And, it was carried out by people who were educated and cultured, people who appreciated good music, art. People who were from good homes and families. Not even ethics can save us, nor the academic analysis of human conduct.

We must celebrate together…we must worship; for it is in worship that we express in strong symbols our inherent love of life, our respect for persons and our reverence for God. It is in worship that we strengthen the sense of the heavenly in us, the sense of something eternal, the sense that there is a judgment of us and all humanity that transcends the judgments for or against us that people or governments make.

Millions died in that classic holocaust. They who were condemned by the Nazi regime are now honored by the world. But the cruel tyrants, the cultured despisers of God and Jews and others whom they regarded as valueless, it is they who are damned.

So it is that we worship to keep our sense of the value of life, of persons, of God alive. We do so, in spite of our troubles, not because we have troubles. We do so even though we know that in one way or another we will all die. Worship is an expression of longing that the murderer will not have the last word.

Prayer

"Your openness to Catholic prayer and tradition at once made me comfortable about studying religion at a Lutheran College and eager to pursue those prayer traditions in my life. Further, your creativity and spontaneity challenged my controlled, overly-ordered posture to open up to life and the gifts and surprises it contains......what a breath of fresh air you were. I certainly see a bit of the Esbj in me when I write a med-itation, take a bus to Central Park, or sing a hymn with unbridled enthusiasm! Ruth, too, has been an inspiration to me, in chapel talks, the friendly face in the library, the hospitality; and your life together, your prayer and close relationship, certainly has made your marriage a sacrament of Christ's love for us." **Monica J. Neal '82**

DJ: As disciplined as Esbj was in worship, so he was in the development of his prayer life. . This sermon delivered on August 9, 1998 (five months after the tornado hit Saint Peter) spells out his core convictions about prayer and tells the story of a turning point in his life when he became even more intensely interested in prayer.

RE: Why do I pray?" I have been doing so since childhood. I pray, though I have suffered losses. My mother died of tuberculosis when she was a young mother, only 30. Illnesses have been a major feature in my family. Heart disease, cancer, diabetes and depression have made life difficult. My wife died of cancer in 1990. My children cope with difficult health problems.

Praying has not prevented suffering. I think about the tornado that struck Saint Peter on March 29, 1998 and caused many people much trouble, including people who pray. Why pray if prayer is not an insurance against disaster?

Why do I pray? And I do even more now than ever. Praying is as essential to me as breathing. It took a long time to realize this. I had to learn a lot about praying to get to this stage where I live prayerfully. I do not pray to live; I live to pray.

A praying life begins in asking for help when we need more resources than we have in order to cope with life's difficulties. Then praying moves to seeking guidance when we are in difficult situations where we have to make decisions but it is not clear as to what we could and ought to do.

At last praying is a matter of being present to God; it becomes an intimate communion with God. Praying out of longing for God's companionship, thirst for God whose love is better than life itself.

It took me a long time to understand this development. Some years ago, in 1973, at the peak of my career as a teacher at Gustavus, I came to realize why

I needed to pray. I had a sabbatical at St. John's Ecumenical Institute in Colleg-eville. I was planning to write a book, for that is what academic people usually do on sabbaticals. They work. In spite of hard work and prayer, I did not suc-ceed. One afternoon, in desolate dismay, I wept for an hour.

Something better happened, because Ruth and I decided to participate in the prayer services with the monks. We chanted the psalms, sang the hymns, listened to the reading from Scripture and other books. We prayed for others as well as ourselves, and we sat in silence.

Praying became the pulse of our lives, matching the beating of our hearts. We learned to understand praying as a way of honoring God, loving God and being loved by God and by those who spend their lives being lovers.

Ruth and I returned to Saint Peter and to our routine lives, but with a differ-ence. We continued the practices we had learned. Every morning after breakfast we prayed, using the psalms, the prayers and the hymns in the *Lutheran Book of Worship*. We read from books, we conversed, we cried and we laughed as we dealt with the difficulties and the delights of our lives.

Then, about 15 years later, Ruth got breast cancer. We continued praying. Two years later the cancer migrated to her brain. We continued praying. During the four remaining months of her life we continued praying. The last act we did together on the night she died was to pray.

Praying did not prevent her suffering and death nor my loss of a good and loving mate. It hadn't prevented my mother's suffering and death either, though she was a devout and praying woman. Praying does not keep us safe from torna-does or terrorist attacks either.

So what is the point of praying? Jesus said, "Ask and you will receive, seek and you will find, knock and it will be opened unto you." Ask, seek, knock. Bold words. Active words.

Ask and you shall receive

Well, we do need all the help we can get. If I have cancer and I pray to be cured, the ravages of cancer may be retarded if it is a prayer of trust rather than of des-peration and fear. There is sufficient evidence to believe that praying can release healing forces natural to our bodies and thus can extend the length of life.

However, the time will come when I must die. I still choose to pray in trust that God knows and provides what I really need in my final time. I need courage to face my mortality. I need courage to commit my life to God, as Jesus did when his final time came.

Asking for help does not get what we think is best, so what do we get? Jesus' words are a clue: "If you then who are evil know how to give good gifts to your children, how much more will your Father in heaven give the *Holy Spirit* to those who ask?" In other words, what God gives in response to our prayers is the inner power to live as well as possible in difficult times. The Holy Spirit is the Comforter, the strength we need to cope with life. The Holy Spirit is the Counselor who gives me wisdom to see that the meaning of my life includes rather than denies the reality of death. The Spirit gives me hope that there is more to life than physical vitality. Asking for benefits stretches our minds, so we gradually learn to discern what is more beneficial than what we wanted. We learn that life is more than food and clothing, and success and prosperity.

Seek and you will find

I do not pray because I want God to reveal my future or the consequences of decisions I might make. Praying is not a form of soothsaying or fortune telling that removes my uncertainty about what is to happen. We need guidance in situations where we don't know what to do and yet cannot avoid making decisions.

Praying is truly a search for understanding . Praying alerts us to the clues we would otherwise miss. Praying shows us ways that seem blocked at first. Praying is trusting God to guide us one decision at a time and to live one day at a time.

The tornado tore up my plans for the future. I wanted to live more simply and so I sold my house and planned to move to an apartment nearby. The tornado damaged that building and scattered my personal property that was stored there.

Now the important question was not "Why me?" but rather "What now?" It was the same question I asked when Ruth died. I continued to pray and I found guidance. I learned to cook, I entertained friends, I traveled, read books and I began a writing occupation. I was in the process of simplifying my life when the tornado hit. Again, I had to ask "What now?" and to pray for guidance. I found another apartment that suited my purposes and needs.

In order to be guided along the right path, we must be open-minded and not set in our ways and angry because we don't get our own way. When we take Jesus' words to heart, praying becomes an adventure as we leave the security and comfort of our conventional ways to search for something we have not yet discovered about ourselves.

By praying we become active participants in a story larger than our own-- God's story unfolding in time. Praying is being responsive to guidance in real-life situations, so that we become co-actors with God.

Knock and It Shall Be Opened

Finally, I learned the most important reason for living prayerfully. It had been the basic reason all along as I prayed for benefits and guidance. I pray because my soul longs for God, my heart thirsts for God, my mind needs wisdom from association with God. I pray to open my heart, mind and soul to the presence of

God. I pray so that I can enjoy the company of God.

In our asking we often encounter silence. In our searching we come to dead ends and closed doors. We come to such places and times and think a relationship with God is closed to us.

As I persisted in praying, I discovered that the love of God is the most valuable treasure we can possess, better than life itself. I learned that the goal of life in our long search for meaning and peace is to enter into that companionship.

I learned that God is present, not absent. So I knock. To pray, said Abraham Hescehl, Jewish philosopher, "is to bring God back into the world, to expand his presence." I would amend that to say that praying is to walk across a threshold into God's world and to expand our awareness of God's presence. The God who hears our prayers is the One who comes to earth to dwell in our vulnerable lives, not as a superhero but as one who suffers with us and for us.

I don't believe that what is on the other side of the door is a safe refuge from the cares of the world. To cross that threshold is an awesome affair in which we surrender our lives and control of our lives. Life on that side of the door is a life of spending our lives, not saving them.

Nevertheless, it is a life so good, so true, so lovely that we do not want to have any other. To live in God's world is to live in love, to be truly in love, truly delighting in others, sharing our mutual benefits and cares, and spending ourselves to be helpful when others are in need.

There is no other God worth loving.

DJ: In another meditation on Luke 11: 5-13, Esbj recounts the story of the man who goes to his neighbor in the middle of the night to ask for a loaf of bread for unexpected company. Usually sermons put the prayer petitioner in the role of the man who comes knocking and asking for bread and the householder in the role of God who can grant the request or not. Esbj gives a surprising twist to the story:

RE: What if, in the story Jesus told, God is the one asking his neighbor for bread for his late-arriving guest? What if the reluctant neighbor is really we who are reluctant to respond but do so because God does not give up in beseeching us? What if…God is asking us for help in attaining his purposes? What if God is working out our salvation for us and depending on us to have active roles in the story? What if God is knocking at the door of our hearts seeking entrance into our lives to transform them into something good and glorious. What if….

Esbj and Tai Chi and Sufi Blessing

DJ: Esbj has a great ability to cross over into other traditions and to take the best of that tradition and adapt it to his own. But Esbj is not just a cross cultural treasure hunter. He has a profound appreciation for what he finds in another culture, honors that culture, learns from it and then brings it home to incorporate it. Therefore, it is not surprising that Esbj practiced Tai Chi nearly every morning. Upon arising, Esbj would face the rising sun out of his eastern picture window on Valley View. Usually he would put on a recording of a psalm or sing his own hymn while doing Tai Chi movements. He did this to enhance his sense of balance and to limber up, but he also used it because the grace of the movement helped center his mind on the grace of life.

Esbj often jogged in the morning when the campus was coming to life. As he went, he often sang a Sufi blessing, inserting the names of persons he knew were working in the campus buildings:

> May the blessings of God rest upon you, Mrs. Young,
> May God's peace abide with you,
> May God's presence illuminate your heart, now and forever more. Amen

What I am Learning About Praying

RE: There was an accumulative force in our participation in the daily worship we experienced at St. John's Abbey during my sabbatical, which we would not have felt if we had visited only occasionally. One evening during the prayers I was struck by recalling that the psalms are ancient songs that have been prayed for centuries. The Benedictines have been praying them for over 1500 years. They had been praying them all those years I was at Gustavus, though I was unaware of it. They would be praying them after I left, and long after I have passed from the Earth there would likely be Benedictines somewhere faithfully praying the offices. I was stepping into a long, long story of prayer and worship linking me to them and to God for just a brief time.

The pulse and rhythm of prayer reminded me of the surf of the Atlantic Ocean crashing on the Cape Cod beach where Ruth and I went for vacations. The breakers, going swish, swish, swish were a steady pulse that has been going on for thousands of years and would go on for eons beyond our lives. We were there for just a brief flick of time, participating in something more lasting than we are. The rhythm of the sea was healing and humbling, and so was the rhythm of the prayers at St. John's Abbey.

Now I hear and say and sing the psalms and other prayers as the pulse of the spirit, going on constantly and into which I consciously enter regularly. They link our lives to a larger life, our stories to a larger story, the story of God's people and the story of God.

Letters From the Edge, Series 1, No. 2, September 26, 1999

Prayer and Eating

I have learned to eat meditatively--to think about the food I eat as life given for my life-the grains, fruits, meats and the human labor that goes into the food on my table are sacrifices to benefit me, so that my life in turn can be spent for others. Try as I might to be so reflective, I find myself gulping food too fast and too thoughtlessly. Eating meditatively is eating thankfully, appreciating what I eat.

Living a Praying Life, Series 2, No. 7, October, 1999

Praying is Like Marriage. Two people make love in all that they do together. The praying life is loving God in all that we do. Praying is communing with God, just as in a marriage two people communicate intimately and intensely and honestly. As in sexual intercourse when two people literally bare themselves to each other, so in praying we become naked in the presence of God. God knows us and we know God. The knowledge is intimate and revealing, it is honest; nothing is hidden. I use the masculine gender usually when referring to God, but a feminine gender is appropriate too; I experience God as mother, one who embraces me, one who surrounds me as a mother's arms cradle her child. That feminine aspect of a praying life is more intimate than the masculine, just as a mother-child is more intimate than a father-child.

More and more I experience praying as a love affair. I pray to keep in touch with God, TO PAY ATTENTION TO GOD.

Living a Praying Life, Series 2, No. 7, October, 1999

Esbj as Proclaimer of The Word

"As president, I was always refreshed by your chapel meditations. They were a charming blend of poetry, deep social concern, Biblical insights, and a measure of whimsy at times. You could be relied on to catch the unusual nuances of a Biblical text and to point out the unexpected applications of it." Edgar M. Carlson, 1983 letter

DJ: Esbj's values and much of his thinking on matters of faith and social concerns are preserved in his sermons and chapel talks. Here is a sampling. Some are full-length and others are excerpted and edited. His sermons are examples of imagination, the creation of images, honesty, comfort and challenge. Esbj was one who struggled (literally) with the Word and the context in which it was to be delivered. His Saturday nights were restless as he processed what he was to say the next day. Indeed, he wrestled all week with the text. Then, his habit was to rise at 4:00 a.m. and put his thoughts on paper. Thus, his thoughts were fresh.

Personal Peace
July 21, 1995
Text: John 20: 19-30

RE: A friend writes in a letter:

What a beacon this church is in this community, one of the few crystals of quality you can count on. It is the Word and the ideals and values contained in it that binds us together, in a thin, invisible network of friendships, the committed church.

Do you agree? Why do we come together other than to hear the Word, the values and ideals in it? To hear the Word about justice. To be encouraged to live in a world that is in so many ways unjust. There is another word that draws me, and very likely you. *Peace.*

Hear the words of Psalm 85:

"I will hear what the Lord has to say, a voice that speaks of peace, peace for his people and his friends, and those that turn to him with their hearts."

Mercy and faithfulness have met, justice and peace have embraced. Peace be within your walls, for the sake of my relatives and friends I will say, Peace be within you. The God of peace be with you all.

There was a meeting on the evening of the first day of the week, the day when Jesus was raised from the dead by the power of the Spirit. The meeting was in a house behind locked doors, because the ones gathering were afraid, afraid because Jesus had been executed, afraid because they feared they would be next.

Jesus came and stood among them and said, "Peace be with you...." That is the message to the despairing, fearful and guilt-burdened followers that gathered in that room behind locked doors. There was no demand for confession of sins, or for a promise to live a better life, simply "peace be with you." Peace is not earned; it is a gift of God. It is very liberating to know we have a merciful God who forgives us, a living Lord who blesses us with the word of peace. We are set free from the burden of guilt.

Peace is a heart condition. It is serenity, like coming into a sheltered, sunlit garden, out of the busy traffic of a city. A load lifted, as at the end of a portage, rest. A freedom from anxiety and stress.

Why do we need to hear the word of peace? Because we are not at peace with ourselves. We can't get through a week without making mistakes, forgetting something, or doing something against what we know is right. We can scarcely get through a day without kicking ourselves for something or other that we have thought, said, or done. We have to make decisions before we are ready, before we have enough information or wisdom to make good decisions, so we are uneasy, not at peace, before we make them, and after as well. We experience failure and defeat, so we feel badly about ourselves.

Why do we need to hear the word, peace? Because in our lives we have to cope with conflicts, with competing demands, in our families, our town, our nation. We live in a nation that resorts to weapons and to violence, so as taxpaying citizens we are shareholders in violence, while at the same time we want the safety that the police force promises.

Jesus said, "My peace I give unto you, not as the world gives it, do I give it." How does the world give peace? Two ways, one is political and the other is psychological.

The political way is to keep the peace by strength, superior power that suppresses and controls the violence and disruption, strong police force, and superior weapons--for which we pay a high price in tax dollars.

The psychological strategy for peace within our psyches is by rationalization. We blame others, and excuse ourselves, in order to ease the burden of guilt.

I am not satisfied with either the political or psychological methods of attaining peace. By force we may suppress the violence only for a time but violent use of force only breeds conditions for more violence. By rationalization we repress the guilt into deep places of our personalities, and so there is an inner war that drains our energies.

Here, in church, we hear about another way to peace. "In quietness and confidence shall be your strength. In trust and faithfulness shall be your peace." We come into the presence of a gracious God, when we come here; or better, we are reminded here that we live daily and everywhere in the presence of a God of steadfast mercy.

One of my students told a story about herself that illustrates this. One Sunday when she was little, the pastor invited the children to gather around him for the children's story. Her parents urged her to go, so she went. But she was scared and shy. The pastor noticed her and said, "Mary, come and sit with me." He took her in his lap while he told the story. Mary said, "That day changed how I felt about the minister, the church and worship."

The beacon light of the church is the steadfast love of God, made so evident in Jesus Christ our Lord. What our religious tradition is trying to do is to hold each generation next to its heart. Maybe that is what changes us, too, the day when we realize that God holds us silently to his heart, the day when someone loves us with an embrace, or a word of peace, the day when a grandparent is so good to us that we are drawn toward the God they love.

The church is a beacon that shines as brightly as a look of mercy for one another. It shines brightly for all who have sin-sick hearts, or hearts tired of conflict and violence. The beautiful light of a church is the countenance of men and women who are filled with joy by the peace that passes all understanding.

What is next?
December 9, 1984
Text: 2 Peter 3:1-4

DJ: Authors have made a fortune writing books speculating about the end times and giving evidence that we are living in the last days. Against just such writings, Esbj offered a much different and more hopeful look at the future. In this sermon, Esbj posed the question to students who were nearing finals and compared their present anxieties and despair to life itself.

RE: What if these are not the final days, not the end? What if your present trials and tribulations are not the last word, not the final chapter, but only a brief and periodic testing? What if there is the Next, not the End? Next semester, next year and next? What if you have a lifetime ahead of you?

We humans are prone to viewing the future in terms of our most immediate present predicament and past experience, rather than seeing our present situation in relation to what is yet to come, our future. If life is hard, and the struggle taxing and the outcome rather bleak for the time being, we tend to see more of the same ahead for us. What we need is a sense of destiny and direction to keep us going.

This line of thought was started by reading and reflecting on the lesson from 2 Peter 3 about the Day of the Lord.

[3]First of all you must understand this, that in the last days scoffers will come, scoffing and indulging their own lusts [4]and saying, "Where is the promise of his coming? For ever since our ancestors died, all things continue as they were from the beginning of creation!"

[8]But do not ignore this one fact, beloved, that with the Lord one day is like a thousand years, and a thousand years are like one day. [9]The Lord is not slow about his promise, as some think of slowness, but is patient with you, not wanting any to perish, but all to come to repentance. [10]But the day of the Lord will come like a thief, and then the heavens will pass away with a loud noise, and the elements will be dissolved with fire, and the earth and everything that is done on it will be disclosed.

[11]Since all these things are to be dissolved in this way, what sort of persons ought you to be in leading lives of holiness and godliness, [12]waiting for and hastening the coming of the day of God, because of which the heavens will be set ablaze and dissolved, and the elements will melt with fire? [13]But, in accordance with his promise, we wait for new heavens and a new earth, where righteousness is at home.[14]Therefore, beloved, while you are waiting for these things, strive to be found by him at peace, without spot or blemish;

New Revised Standard Version

The author, a second-generation Christian living at the end of the first century, had a problem. Scoffers were ridiculing the teaching of the apostles about the Day of the Lord. The first-generation Christians believed the day was coming soon, even within their own lifetime. The author refers specifically to our "beloved brother Paul," who believed there was not much time left before the Lord would return in glory.

The scoffers were saying, "Where is the promise of his coming? Ever since the fathers fell asleep, all things have continued as they were from the beginning of creation." They were right, weren't they? The Day of the Lord did not come within the lifetime of those who first believed. It is now almost 2,000 years later, and the Day of the Lord has not come. The author attempted an explanation by saying, "With the Lord one day is as a thousand years, and a thousand years as one day. The Lord is patient, forbearing with you, not wishing that any should perish but that all should reach repentance."

What if we are not at the end of human history, but only at the beginning?

What if we humans are not finished but only clumsy beginners in the art of creative living--like seventh grade basketball players or like seven-year-old piano students just beginning?

What if the sufferings of this present time are not worth comparing with the glory that is to be revealed to us? What if our attainment in science and technology and in human relations and organization and in the arts are mere child's play compared to the possibilities of the future?

Consider the changes in the short time since intelligent humans came upon this planet.

Cave-dwelling humans would be utterly astonished by huge, complex cities of our time. They had a hard enough time making the transition to building and living in free-standing huts and houses in small villages. Peasants in the age of archaic agricultural societies would not have been able to imagine genetic manipulation to produce high-yield crops. It was radical enough change to save and plant seeds for next year's crop. The early forms of human organization were crude and cruel compared to the complex and more orderly societies of modern times. It has all happened in a relatively short time. As a matter of personal experience, I could not have imagined genetic manipulation when I was your age: yet it has happened. When we consider the 18-billion-year history of the universe, or the five-billion-year history of the solar system or the two-million-year history of humankind, the history of civilization is very short, and the history of science but a moment, 200 years long.

What lies ahead? It may be so far advanced, even in 100 years, and certainly in a thousand or a million years, that we can hardly imagine it. What if we are not at the end but at the beginning of a long story? Is it not rather arrogant to believe that we are the best generation that could ever be? Is it not rather despairing to think that we are the last generation?

What is the larger and longer story in which our lives are but a tiny episode? One possibility is that the universe is moving toward destruction. That in the end, everything will be destroyed, and there will be nothing, not even time and space. The author of 2 Peter and other writers of scripture present such a vision:

The Day of the Lord will come like a thief, and then the heavens will pass away with a loud noise, and the elements will be dissolved with fire, and the earth and the works that are upon it will be burned up.

This sounds almost modern. Although science provides a variety of scenarios for the fate of the universe, they all involve the demise of the universe as we know it today. To that extent they coincide with most religious eschatology. The first-century Christians could not have known the immense time scale of the future of the universe. The death of the cosmos is so remote as to make it impossible to relate it to human activities. Ah, maybe so, but the end could come to human history, its civilization much sooner. We could have nuclear disasters that would bring on a nuclear winter that would freeze living things to death. Yes, we could.

So, let us consider rewriting 2 Peter 3: "Since all this could happen, what sort of persons ought we to be?" Let us do nothing about tomorrow. Let us live as though there will be no tomorrow. Let us get ours while there is still something to get.

But that vision and that pattern of behavior are not the only alternative. There is another, also hinted at in 2 Peter. Not destruction, but transformation. Not the universe as the final reality but God, the Creator, who makes all things new and does not wish that any should perish and gives us time and space for changing our ways, for repentance. The clue to this alternative is in this line: "But according to his promise we wait for new heavens and a new earth in which righteousness dwells."

This turns out to be a free rewording of a line in Isaiah 65: 17:
"For I am about to create new heavens and a new earth;
  the former things shall not be remembered or come to mind."

Think on this: This vision came over 2500 years ago, near the beginning of civilization – a vision of a world at peace, no infant mortality, no lack of housing or food, people living to an age far older than now, people enjoying the work of their hands, people not laboring in vain, or bearing children for calamity. It is a vision that human despair has not been able to erase. It still persists. It is not a forecast; it is a hope.

That vision survives among a people who believe in the creating God as the final reality. It is this God who creates this universe, and could create another. It is this God who can inspire goodness in humans and the persistence of hope in the dark times of distress. It is this God who gives us this time and place, here on this planet, in this country, on this campus to do what lies before us to do.

What sort of persons ought we to be when we have this hope? People living lives of "holiness and godliness," people "waiting for and hastening or striving for the Day of the Lord."

What may we say about this advice today? What does it mean to have lives of holiness and godliness? For starters, we should be much more careful about using up nonrenewable resources, like cultivatable soil and the precious water reservoirs and oil deposits.

We are spending them as if there was no tomorrow. Are we not called to repent, to change our lifestyles toward a thriftier and simpler and healthier lifestyle? We are called to devote much more of our time on learning to be inventive, creative and forward looking human beings. We need a generation of innovators now more than ever who will come up with appropriate technologies that will provide better housing, food and transportation, and for future development in space. We need, above all, social inventions. We need to devote creative thought to peace-making.

There are so many exciting and challenging tasks ahead of us all, but especially for the young. Put your present efforts learn in the context of this story of creativity and in this climate of hope inspired by ancient writers and those of us who will not let despair control our lives.

It all comes down to the bottom line: What do you and I believe about the final reality? We can choose to live by hope, inspired by the belief that the final reality is a patient, creating, redeeming God whose power can transform all that exists, who brings all things to fulfillment, who has purposes beyond the troubles and tribulations of this present time, whose hope is for new heavens and a new earth, for righteousness.

Which story will be the one you choose to believe? And in which story will you place your own story?

Jesus' Resurrection: Why I Believe.

RE: Behold, I tell you a mystery: Jesus Christ lives still in the lives of believers. Let me put it simply. Every Sunday, at least, we experience the resurrection of Jesus Christ as the people we call the Church gather, for the Church is the body of Christ, his physical presence in the world.

They are the people who are devoted, who believe that the God Jesus reveals can be trusted and who are inspired by a living hope that cannot be taken away from them. I used to stand at the window in the narthex of the church in Judson, a town up the valley, and watch the people come to church, and I was overwhelmed by the wonder of it.

They were Christ's body. They were my physical evidence that Jesus Christ was alive. It was those ordinary people, along with some of the great and famous Christians I had come to know, who dispelled my depression, despair and doubts.

People who also knew the threat of death, who like me had disillusioning and disappointing experiences, and who like me (and the disciples) had defected from their dedication. Yet, they came, drawn still by the power of Jesus Christ. It is ordinary people, like the disciples, and like us, that become the body of Christ, who know his risen life in our own lives.

Honors Day at Lystra (undated)

DJ: "Honors Day at Lystra" was delivered the day after Honors Day at Gustavus.

More than once I heard Esbj lament the fact that many Gustavus graduates live honorable, servant-type lives and are never recognized for their invaluable contributions. He spoke of the mothers at home, the social workers, the community volunteers, and others in low- paying work who labor faithfully and, in terms of recognition by the College that prepared them and inspired them to a life of service, would never be celebrated with a Distinguished Alumni Citation. He was thinking of Emerson Engberg, son of Professor and Mrs. Emmer Engberg of Gustavus. Emerson, a brilliant student, suffered some mental impairment as a result of an automobile crash. Emerson became a volunteer at the Augustana Church in Washington, D.C. Esbj lamented, "he will never achieve the honors that otherwise might have been his." He may also have been thinking about his daughter, Louise, who as a result of chronic illness and resultant mental and emotional struggles, never fulfilled her bright promise. He specifically cites, in this chapel talk, an alumnus of the College who works as a teacher's aid in an institution for the mentally handicapped.

The text is from Acts 14:5-20. It is the story of Paul and Barnabas healing a cripple in the city of Lystra.

RE: The College recognized some beautiful people on Saturday. They are bright achievers in research, service and scholarship. And it is right so to do. A college should honor its brightest and best. It was a marvelous day demonstrating to all the high achievements of our students.

The counterpoint to Gustavus Honors Day is honors day at Lystra. Paul gave an award; it was not to an achiever, but to a believer. We don't know the man's name. He was a cripple. He had never walked. Perhaps he had a genetic defect. Perhaps he was crippled by lack of proper nutrition in his infancy. Nonetheless, Paul recognized him. Paul saw belief in his eyes, on his face. This man believed the Good News that Paul proclaimed in Lystra. So Paul said to him, "Stand upright on your feet." He sprang up and walked. This caused quite a commotion. Paul had a knack for that. Finally the tables were turned and the crowd wanted to stone Paul and Barnabas. That was the end of Lystra's Honors Day.

The juxtaposition of this story and our Honors Day started me thinking. Could we have a "Faith Award" in memory of the cripple who believed in the Good News? Probably not, yet, there is an award for faith. The award is intrinsic. The reward of faith is liberation.

A faithful person is a free person. Free to walk upright. Free to be himself, whatever inherited limitations he has. Free from the mad belief that one must be a god. Free to be human, to have human feelings. Free to love. Free to be thankful, Free to see God's goodness in the rain and the grain. Free from sadness. And free for gladness of heart.

I began to think of all the not-honored people at Gustavus. They remain unnamed, unlisted, unrecognized. They have average records. They do not get research or teaching fellowships. Some of them will not get jobs that correspond to their training or aims.

What does Gustavus say to them? They know they, like the crippled man, are not the achievers, not beautiful, not brilliant. Handicapped by bad habits or broken homes, by depression or heartbreaks, by limited backgrounds or genetic defects, they do not make the dean's list. What can be said to them? I have Good News on a Monday. Good news of a living and loving God who liberates those who believe, so that they can make the most of their lives.

During Easter break my wife and I stopped at another institution located in central Nebraska. It is called Bethphage. It is a home for the physically and mentally handicapped. We wanted to visit a college friend, a Gustie, who has lived there for quite a few years. He is a teacher's aid, working with people who can scarcely learn anything.

Nathan is a free man, dear Gusties--not because he can do anything he wants, which he can't. But because he can believe in his own worth, because he believes in the worth of his obscure, unrecognized service, and believes in a living and loving God. Nathan has heard Paul's Good News. He is an avid reader of the Bible. Nathan will not be given an alumni award. He is not an achiever. He cannot do much in the competitive world. But Nathan is a believer. I honor him on Monday after Honors Day, not with praise of him, but praise of God, the living and loving God who has liberated Nathan to serve the least who are out of sight and out of mind.

Do you question the validity of Christians going about stirring up commotions (as Paul and Barnabas did) by trying to convert people? Paul meant no put-down of other religions and traditions, but he was a messenger with good news and when one has good news, it has to be published. I am wondering what would have happened to Nathan if he had never heard the Good News? I wonder if the mongoloids and the cripples and the others there in that tiny town in Nebraska would be served as they are?

I am glad that Nathan and the others are there to be benefactors for the least of these--the marginal people of our society. I am glad they do not have to die without hope, or love or faith. Thinking about Bethphage, which some call "the miracle on the prairie," I am glad for Christ Chapel. Paul's good news comes alive for all of us, too, for honor students and those who are not honor students. To know that God lives and loves through his servants satisfies our hearts with gladness.

O crippled man of Lystra, you have made our hearts glad. Thanks be to God, who lives and loves and liberates. May we pass on the Good News that generations unborn may hear and believe and set all free.

"On being a Christian subversive"

DJ: From a sermon to his flock in Bethany Lutheran Church, in nearby Judson, sometime during the Cold War. Text: words from Jeremiah and Jesus (Luke 19:41-44) about the "things that make for peace."

RE: He comes to us from across the years and says: Robert, you are a pastor, a shepherd. Your job is to care for the unwanted, the undesirable, those who have lost their way, the oppressed. I have deputized you to carry on my work. If you turn things backward and use the work to better yourself, you have turned Bethany into a den of robbers. You are a robber. Our nation has spent 10 times as much on warfare and related programs as it has on human welfare. That is official violence.

The first thing that makes for peace is to repent our unthinking worship of military might. Do not trust in horses because they are many, said Isaiah. Do not trust in missiles and militia because they are many, I say.

The second thing that makes for peace is to repent of our unrestrained worship of economic growth. The god of production society is GNP, not GOD. We must stop producing just anything and reorder our priorities so as to reflect a more conservationist sense of value. We must be willing to pay for recreation space for the public, we must be willing to pay for clean water and air. We must take up again the charge God gave us to manage the Earth properly for the welfare of all living things.

A third thing that makes for peace is respect of persons. We must abolish those blinding prejudices that prevent us from seeing people who are different as persons. Particularly we must repent of race prejudice and prejudice against Russians. We must be willing to recognize and rejoice in diversity and see our common humanity.

Finally, the basic condition of peace is true rather than false religion. True religion is to believe that God wants justice and peace, that God is the Father of all mankind and a special advocate and protector of widows, the poor and the oppressed. True religion is to believe that devotion to him is expressed in actions that are in keeping with that belief.

We have a very good congressman, Ancher Nelsen, in the sense that he listens to his constituents. He votes as he thinks his constituents want. He dismisses critics as insignificant because so many in his district are apparently in favor of the existing military system, growth economy and its perilously high hidden expenses and policies prejudicial against minority groups. We prefer private goods to public improvements.

If Ancher Nelsen would hear a different tune from his constituents, he would support more readily the things that make for peace. He is a good and reasonable man. You should write to him. He thinks you accept everything that is going on.

Remember these words from Jeremiah: "The days are coming when your enemies shall surround you and dash you to the ground--you and your children, because you did not know the time of your opportunity. If you do not act, your children and your children's children will despise your memory."

Faith and Culture.

RE: Faith is the audacity to believe that the cultural idolatries of the present are not trustworthy. Faith is the readiness to challenge the conventional wisdom of a particular society.

Esbj and Abortion

DJ: In this essay, Esbj lays out the moral dilemma of abortion. In the midst of all the angry debate, Esbj asks us not to forget the woman herself who bears the burden. He points us to both "evangelical freedom and burden" and the liberating word of forgiveness. It is also an example of Esbj's focus on the person in ethical dilemmas rather than on principles.

A Woman in Trouble (1981)

Text: Luke 6: 36-50

RE: One of the many difficult dilemmas that cannot be resolved by moral or legal or medical judgments is the plight of the woman who finds that she is pregnant when she does not want to be. She may be a forty-year-old mother of three who runs a high risk of bearing a child with Down Syndrome.

She may be a wretched, poor woman in Santiago, Chile, where it has been estimated that there are two abortions for every live birth among the poor people. She may be a college senior with a graduate school career planned. She may be your roommate. She may be your son's girlfriend. She could be you. For whoever it is, the plight offers no simple, right answer. Either to terminate the pregnancy or to carry to term, both are fraught with difficult consequences. There is no easy solution.

The liturgical calendar today honors Pastor Theodore Fleidner's work during the last century. Pastor Fleidner and his wife lived in a destitute German parish. They cared about unwed mothers. They cared about women criminals. They cared about unwanted children. They cared about women displaced by the shift from rural to urban living conditions. I began to think about the plight of many women in our changing society, and especially about the growing number of women who must decide whether or not to have an abortion.

Our text today is about the bad woman whose affectionate ministry was accepted by Jesus--in the midst of a dinner party, no less. Let us put in that woman's place a woman who has had an abortion! Dare she approach Jesus? This woman knows her genetics. She knows that it is a human life that would one day be a baby in her arms that is killed by an abortion. She knows in her deepest thoughts that no euphemism can change that biological fact. And she knows that she is no neo-Nazi maliciously ready to murder an unwanted baby. She is a person caught in a moral bind from which there is no easy escape. To terminate a pregnancy is hard. To carry to term is a rocky road.

There may be some women who justify themselves, but few who escape the troubling consequences, and none who escape the emotional pain of conflict between the natural desire to be a mother and the fear and rejection of an untimely pregnancy. Barbara Ward, devout Roman Catholic and renowned economist wrote, *The sacredness of life is involved…the dilemma is that we are faced with a choice of evils. Abortions occur in a torrent, in a cataract of misery around the world.*

About 26 to 35 million abortions a year are performed. Illegal abortion means poor women go to criminal abortionists. The hospitals then take the battered, poisoned consequences of these vile operations. For the rich, the safe, quiet clinic is usually available. Ward continued:

It is the miserable, the poor, the ignorant and the frightened who carry in septicemia, in maimed bodies, in agony and death, the consequences of illegal operations in filthy conditions down back streets. There is no good answer between the principle involved in legalizing what is a form of (killing) and the practice involved in leaving wretched women with no recourse save to criminal and hence hidden, incompetent and medically disastrous illegal practitioners…the world will not necessarily be a more evil place as a result of legalizing abortions. You many comfortable Christians have turned a blind eye to the realities of abortion among the majority of the world's people who are desperately poor.

The text today comes from the past into the present to make us think hard about troubled women today. Reading it is to experience a confrontation with Him who accepted the affectionate attentions of and gave respect and forgiveness to a fallen woman.

In the Fleidner story we watch the Christ story continued. He was a man who cared as Christ cared and drew around him deaconesses, who found a meaningful alternative to an uprooted, lonely life in Germany's new industrial society by service on behalf of the sick, the unwanted children and other needy people who were outcasts.

We have an encounter with Christ whenever we meet one of the doctors, nurses, pastors and other workers in human services who care deeply about women facing the painful dilemma brought upon them by an unexpected and undesired pregnancy and participate in helping them make their hard decisions about abortions.

Can we believe that this Christ inspires shouts of condemnations: Murderer. Nazi.

Do we forget that a woman cannot get pregnant alone? Do we forget that it is she and not the man who must decide whether or not to go to an abortion clinic? Do we forget that it is she in whom the conflict between the natural thrill of being a mother and the anxiety about her future and about exposure to angry, hurt or judgmental people is a tearing pain?

I do not ask, "Do you approve her pregnancy?" I do not ask, "Do you approve of her decision to have an abortion?" I do ask, myself and you, "Where would we be in a social occasion at which a woman known to have had an abortion is present?" I do ask, "What would we think if she stood next to us at the altar where we celebrate in the Holy Feast the memory of the forgiving Christ. Would we be among those who are a Christ-like presence in her life at a time of deep personal distress? Would she be able to find some party where her feelings could be released, her tears flow, her self-respect restored by forgiving words, by accepting friends, by the promise of a new beginning and an open future?

She must decide to abort or carry to term what grows within her. The law permits her to choose. Her church's statement, if she belongs to the Lutheran Church in America, gives her "evangelical freedom" to decide. But instead of relief she suffers the bitter taste of anxiety which is the burden of freedom of a person who must make her own decision. It is impossible to justify one's action by appeal to the law in any satisfactory way. At the moral level she falls short of the glory of God, as we all do. In life and death dramas, such as these, the test is not of one's moral integrity, but of one's faith, of how we stand before God.

What manner of God? Not a God of death but of life. A God who gives what is needed for life, for wholesome fullness of life. God whom we know in Christ does not demand either the life of the mother or the child as a sacrifice for some principle that is outside the existence of the person.

She discovers no escape from the test question, "What is the loving act--not only love for her own person but for the person who might be and for generations yet to come?" There is a perspective that can keep hope that will never disappoint alive, hope that she can experience joy even now in her trials and troubles. She hears the Word of a God who raised from the dead the Lord Jesus Christ who was delivered to death for her sins and raised again to secure her justification. She hears a word promising her a new relationship of grace, the promise of a new beginning, of mature character and a new life born in the agony of the death of her old life in a fate she did not intend.

No one can tell her what to do. Her physician cannot, nor her pastor, nor her bishop, nor her parents, nor her friends. We know that it is none of us that she must fear and love, but God.

With such a God, the woman can with confidence draw near to the throne of grace and ask God to help her in her hour of need. That word cancels the condemnation and proclaims the pardon and the promise that God can make good come from a pregnancy continued or terminated.

Whatever she decides, we can invite her to join the rest of us forgiven sinners in a song of thanksgiving for the words, "Your sins are forgiven. Your faith has saved you. Go in peace."

Esbj and Women, 1982

DJ: Esbj was quick to provide leadership to a new understanding of the relationship between men and women. In a 1982 sermon given in New Ulm, Minnesota, Esbj preached on the text about a woman who broke the rules and approached Jesus, even though she was "unclean." He uses other examples of how women were treated as "second class" in their society.

RE: Is there any more devastating evidence of sin and its consequences than the persistence of subjugation of women and the perversion of the relationship between women and men. Jesus was a liberator and the most basic liberation is in this most fundamental relationship. We have yet to catch up with Jesus! The story may be old, but it is still an innovation when we juxtapose that society with the trite, tedious stereotyped pattern of domination and subjugation that still persists in our society, as evident in the resistance to the Equal Rights Amendment.

Esby and the Environment

DJ: In many sermons, Esbj both "sounded the alarm" and set forth the cure to our environmental ills, which the reader will by now understand are the twin principles of worship and care of the Earth. For Esbj the two cannot be separated. He illustrates this in a chapel talk about his imaginary conversation with St. Francis just prior to the 1989 Nobel Conference on the theme of "The End of Science?" The text is Psalm 148

Saint Francis Walks Again!

RE: Francis of Assisi walked into my world again last Friday, as he has in the past, about the time of the Nobel Conference. St. Francis Day, October 4, and Nobel Days often coincide.

I was walking alone, enjoying a beautiful fall day, humming a tune, "Come, walk with Francis," and thinking about him.

"Roberto"

Mamma mia, there he was, again.

"I have been cruising around campus, Roberto."

"You came early this year. It's only September 29."

"The director of the Nobel Conference--what is his name? Riccardo?--took my day away again for Nobel."

"What is your message to us, Francesco, this year?"

94

"Your conference is about the end of science! Hungry one morning, I followed some students into a room called the Three Crowns and had some rolls and juice. I stayed to listen to a more or less dignified conversation about the end of science, led by two professors."

"I was there, Francesco, I didn't see you."

"I kept a low profile, Roberto. I felt very much the outsider."

"It's no wonder, Francesco. You dropped through a wrinkle in time from the age of religion, which ended centuries ago, some people think. We are living in an age of science, and in that age you really are an anomaly, strange, odd, and disturbing."

"Roberto, one of the professors spoke as if he believed that the age of science may be at an end. I do not understand this. How can anything true end?" I tried to explain post-modern man to him, but my effort fell flat.

"Roberto, I have been thinking about the end of science in another way, not its demise but its purpose."

"Very good, Francesco. I hope that meaning of the word will affect the discussion at the Nobel Conference."

He asked me if I had read something about his ideas in the papers recently. I said that I didn't remember anything about him. He pulled a clipping out of his cowl and read it to me. It was about humans as threats to nature. I recognized the author, Ellen Goodman. It was about how humans are so numerous and aggressive that there is hardly a place on Earth untouched by human manipulation, about how even the very weather is being changed by human action, by smog and pollution, how we are making a greenhouse out of a wild garden. It was about deep ecology, about limits and restraints, about a warning that nature, the independent force that has surrounded us since our earlier days, cannot coexist with our numbers and our habits. The last paragraph said, "Nature is already pushed back to prairie museums, zoos, national parks, protected species....If we don't limit our numbers, and our habits, all we'll have of nature will be on videotapes."

Francis sighed and said, "What a sad and dull world this would be if all creatures of our God and King were expelled from their worlds by human domination. That would be the end of nature! Is that the end of science to banish nature?"

"No, no, Francesco! Many scientists are very disturbed about what is happening to our environment. You have to understand what motivates scientists. It is curiosity, Francesco, they have a love affair with knowledge. That passion drives scientists to explore everything, everywhere."

"And control, Roberto, control. You modern people want to control nature, and conquer it, and you get a big assistance from scientists."

"I admit as much." Francis said he overheard someone refer to him as the patron saint of ecology, so he wanted to know what ecology was. I said it was the science of whole systems in which all living creatures and their environments are interacting and interdependent.

"What has that to do with me?" Francis asked.

"People think you had a great reverence for nature, and that this attitude must replace the exploitation of nature before we completely ruin the planet."

Francis stopped me. "Roberto! What has happened to the feeling of kinship--with sun and moon, with water and all that swims in it, with the birds...to a sense of great joy and delight, such as we have for people we love." Then he began to sing his canticle, out loud, right in front of Trinity Church and Saint Peter's across the street. "Praised be you, My Lord, for all your creatures, especially by Sir Brother Sun who makes the day and through whom you give us light." I joined in and we sang a few verses. Suddenly Francis stopped. "What do you hear?"

"You call the sun *brother*, and the moon *sister*, and water and birds--to everything you give titles of intimate relationships in the family. You obviously have a great sense of kinship with other living beings."

"I am not praising the sun, the moon, the birds. I am praising God."

"I know. You are not worshiping the creatures. You are praising God for them, because you love them as if they were your own kin."

"You are not Italian, Roberto. Let me sing a line in Italian." When he finished, he said,

"There is one word that is important in my song. The word *per*; it can mean both *for* and *by* . I praise God for brother sun and all the other creatures, but I am also singing, "Praised be you, my Lord, *by* them. Psalm 148, Roberto, look it up when you get home."

When I arrived home, I read Psalm 148. Francis was right. The psalmist called on all creatures to join him in praising God. I decided to make that the text for today's chapel talk.

Praise the Lord! Praise him, sun and moon, praise him, all you shining stars.

Praise the Lord from the earth, you sea monsters, fire and hail, mountains, beasts, kings of the earth, young men and maidens, old men and children.

Francis came to me again last night. "Come, walk with me," he said. He took me through a wrinkle in time into the future. It was a future where humans and tiny robots looking very much like a Walkman co-mingled. There were many. They lived in huge plastic bubbles, like Buckminster Fuller's geodesic dome, because the atmosphere outside was too hot and dirty. Humans, with the help of robots, produced food without either farmers or farms. We saw no birds or animals anywhere. When we asked about them, one of the humans tolds us about the Ecozoos, so we went to one of them. People stood in long lines to go in and stare for a few minutes at colonies of baboons and other creatures.

Nature was banished! The dire prediction had come true! We hastened out. Somewhere we heard singing. The tune was familiar. The music was coming from another building, so we joined the humans in it, and this was the song we heard:

"Praised be you. O Lord Homosap, by all the computers, by IBM and Apples, Amigas and NeXTs through whose work we have mastered our world. Praised be you, O Lord Homosap, by all cameras and satellites, by all video-and audiotapes. You are our children. Praise you the Lord. Praised be you, O Lord Homosap, by all medications by Sominex and zanex, barbituates and Benadryl, aspirin and Nuprin. You are our children. Praise you the Lord."

Who, we wondered, was the "Lord--the praised?" Who was Lord Homosap?

Francis looked at me. There were tears in his eyes. I felt very sad and scared. Would this be the world of my descendants, a world from which both nature and nature's Lord would be banished, leaving only *homo sapiens*?

The vision ended. I was in my writing chair. And now, I am here, in this Christ Chapel pulpit. I invite you to come, walk with Francis, in the way of praise of God, for and with all God's creatures. Come, walk with Francis, in the way of poverty, of radical trust in God's providence. Come, walk with Francis, In the way of peace, contentment, courtesy and compassion. Come, pray with Francis. Come, sing with Francis! Praised be…

Who Killed Kitchigami?

DJ: Esbj wrote this poem in April of 1970. Kitchigami is an Ojibwe word meaning " big or many waters," referring to Lake Superior.

> I never would have dreamed
> When I was young
> Of Kitchigami's death.
> Sooner would the sky fall down
> Than that lake die,
> In whose cold, clear depths
> The large trout lie.
> How could I have guessed
> That my desires
> Multiplied a trillion times
> Would soon deplete the iron mines
> By Lake Vermillion,
> Or that automated giants,
> Eating the earth's more modest ores,
> Would pellets make

And tailings to pollute that lovely lake?
How blue and clear it was in those days
When I was young and saw that Lake
So far away as I gazed
And dreamed of Easterness
Before our land was razed
By greed and bitterness.

Pandora's Box, 1970 Model

Earth Day, April 22, 1970

My announced topic is open to several prognostications as to what my speech will stress.

As you know, there is a Siamese cat in the Esbjornson home called Pandora. And, she has a box. And she pollutes it. Better that than the living room rug.

What I have said to you is a parable. He who has ears to hear, let him hear. And be not as the man who hearing, understands nothing.

There is also a Greek myth about a woman named Pandora, the first mortal woman, sent by Zeus as a punishment to mankind for the theft of fire by Prometheus. Zeus gave her a box which she opened, letting out all human ills into the world--or (in a latter version) letting all human blessings escape and be lost, leaving only hope.

That myth has possibilities, too. At the risk of being ostracized by the Women's Liberation Movement, I would suggest that while men gave us technology, women gladly use its benefits to the point that human safety and serenity are lost, as the nuisances in our lives increase and the dire costs to our finite environment escalate.

The consumer is the ultimate culprit, and the American consumer is very convenience-oriented, and female, according to statistics. So the myth reminds us that man *and*_woman, producer and consumer, are in Pandora's box together.

What is left to us is *hope*. There is still time. The question is, what do we do about the shrinking of options left open to us to restore the blessings in the one Pandora's box and reduce the pollution in the other?

Esbj's Prairie Overlook Blessing

DJ: In 1993, In honor of Chester Johnson's 80th birthday, the Chester and Marian Johnson family gave "The Prairie Overlook and Boulder Circle" to Linnaeus Arboretum. This gift honors and celebrates the presence of the Peterson/Swanson/Johnson families on the Gustavus campus for nearly 100 years. The gift is also their endorsement of Gustavus' commitment to environmental values in higher education, the preservation of the vanishing prairie, and the stewardship of the land.

Johnson is emeritus professor of geology, a neighbor of the Esbjornsons and faculty colleague. The following meditation and blessing was written by Robert Esbjornson for the dedication of the "Prairie Overlook" on October 30, 1993.

RE: We may very well be recapitulating an ancient habit of creating places for rituals of remembrance, so with this Ritual of Dedication, we need a story..... one from the book of Joshua, Chapter 4, verses 5 to 7 (*New Revised Standard Version*).

Joshua said to the tribes of Israelites: "Pass on before the ark of the Lord your God into the middle of the Jordan, and each of you take up a stone on his shoulder, one for each of the tribes so that this may be a sign among you. When your children ask in time to come, 'What do those stones mean to you?' then you shall tell them that the waters of the Jordan were cut off in front of the ark of the covenant of the Lord. When it crossed over the Jordan, the waters of the Jordan were cut off. So these stones shall be to Israelites a memorial forever.

Our actions today make this a marked place, no longer an anonymous piece of prairie. It will be a place set apart, where we can stand on a rock higher than the prairie, or sit quietly on a silent stone, letting it stun us into a silence as still as it is, waiting for a word speaking its message, until we hear the ancient sounds of its journey under a mountain of ice a mile high, echoing down the slopes of time, thousands of years, still echoing. Silent until the geologist teaches the stones to talk. Geologists are their priests, giving the stones names and messages, telling their stories. Telling us there is something deeper here than fertile prairie soil, something way down deep.

Stones are down there somewhere, symbols of the depth, depths of time reminding us how young we are, how short our time, how soon we will pass away, like the grass. We may even hear the stones giving the same message to our children's children, years and years from now, for these stones will outlast us. The stones are teaching us to number our days humbly, teaching us that there is more to the ground on which we stand than meets the eye, and more to living than words can tell. Teaching us to know that the stones are made of star dust, the stuff of all creation, as we are, too. Teaching us to be wonderers, awed by the mute silence, the ancient shapes, the vast forces that made them, teaching us to understand better the language of faith, which sees God as a rock, a strong place where we can take our stand.

We will come here, some of us often, to listen to the rocks, to meditate on the splendor of God, the strength of that which is deep and invisible and silent. And so we dedicate this place with a prayer, that in some ways past our knowledge it may be a blessed place, will be in some way a healing place, amid the beauty of the prairie flowers, and the birds that sing. A place where the still, small voice of the eternal God may come and teach us to number our days, and to seek wisdom, combining truth and love. O God, our Creator, loving us into being, make it so. Amen.

Esbj and A Culture of Life

"The year was 1967. Your chapel talks, ethics courses, trip to Chicago's inner city and vision for Riverbend were already in my consciousness. But these experiences were being distorted by a war which was sorely dividing our country. If Gustavus students had been apathetic, they would no longer remain so. A growing number of us saw the contradictions and felt strongly that it was time to take a stand. Campus activism flared up almost overnight. You were understandably concerned that we may have been moving too quickly. On the eve before our campus teach-in, you challenged me to think about what we were doing and with encouragement gave me the opportunity to articulate my convictions. Then at the teach-in, you joined in by speaking out with all your heart and might. The next morning you handed me a cash contribution to support the trip to Washington and the group's non-violent march to the Pentagon. You believed in me and my sincerity and about what some of us had decided to do. Your gesture was a touching and affirming moment for me and I shall never forget it." **Dick Little '68**

DJ: Esbj was a man of peace. For him, peace was a way of life, a natural response to a loving God, a loving Creator and a good creation. He spoke on behalf of humankind from his own small corner of the world. Most of what follows are excerpted from sermons.

On the Nuclear Threat

RE: It was Yahweh who made the promise never again to strike down every living thing, not Noah. The Yahwist historian of the Davidic monarchy never dreamed that one day humans would have this power. Is it not high time that we humans answer the Lord God with our own promise, never to destroy life on this planet? 1982

Most of all, I will recall reading your personal words of encouragement as I sat in my cell in King County Jail. It moved me to overflowing that you could identify with me and see the reasons for my civil disobedience, and understand the roots for it out of our common faith. **Jon Nelson '55 arrested 1985 for protesting the Trident nuclear sub-marine**

One Antidote to the Madness of War

DJ: While laying out the threat that nuclear weapons and warmongering are to human life, Esbj asks how can we touch the hearts of people? His response:

RE: To inspire commitment we need to raise our level, not only of the comprehension of the danger we face, but also of sensitivity to the goodness and beauty of life. This calls us to contemplation. Contemplation is as essential as action. It is contemplation of the wonders of life on this planet, of the wonder of human beings, of the wonder of intelligence, of the wonder of caring to which we are called. This means that the Sabbath must be observed more faithfully, where we are engaging in the praise of life, intelligence and caring and most surely in whatever quiet circle, quiet time and quiet way you find for being attentive to the God who gives the gift of life, and intelligence and love. 1984

Standing Against the Gods of Death

DJ: I Kings 17:8-16 records the story of the widow with dwindling resources (one cruse of oil and one cake of bread). A stranger, Elijah, asks her for something to eat. She declines as she is saving a last meal for herself and her son. Elijah persists promising her that the cruse of oil shall not be spent and the jar of meal shall not fail until God sends rain again. The woman trusts, shares what she has and all three live. Esbj's sermon follows:

RE: The story is a legend. Its point is not that God steps into scenes of natural and human disaster with magical solutions. God is not a magician. Such a view of God dies every day that people die of hunger and violence in spite of their prayers.

The point of the story is a more striking, awesome wonder--the woman's faith in a promise, not at a time when she had plenty to spare, but when she was down to the last meal and confronting imminent death.

There is a reality greater than death and also greater than life. We call that reality the Lord God of Sabaoth, the Creator who calls us to be his own, live under him in his kingdom, and serve him in everlasting righteousness, innocence and blessedness. If we cease to honor and fear, love and trust in God above all things, we cease to be. We die before we die. We become pawns of death, vulnerable to the control of death-dealers. And then we soon join them, protecting what we think as our turf amidst our dwindling resources.

The threat of joblessness, hunger and war are immanent for millions of us. We are moving toward the last quart of oil and the last bushel of wheat--like the widow. And there she stands, in the shadow of death, like a luminous presence, with her last cruse in one hand and a cake for us in the other. She is a model of trust in the promise of God. That trust is the well spring of generosity, of willingness to share from even the little we have with widows, orphans, and even foreigners.

This may turn out to be the most practical way to forestall the "final non-solution" of nuclear annihilation. 1982

Esbj, 1996.

Chapter Seven

Esbj and the Writing Life

DJ: Esbj was a prolific writer. Yet, he did not publish much as a faculty member. That seemed difficult for him to do. He describes his anguish and his failures.

RE: I have prayed for years for guidance about invitations I have had to submit something I have written for publication. In 1950, I was taking a course in Christianity and Politics at Yale University. I chose the career of then Governor Luther Youngdahl of Minnesota for my master's thesis in political ethics. After my arrival at Gustavus I worked on it over a period of four years, while teaching a full course load and preaching every Sunday. After I got my degree in June, Ren Anderson, public relations director at Gustavus, read it and showed the manuscript to Lawrence Brings of Denison Press. Brings said he would publish it if I would revise it to include more biographical material.

The book was launched at a signing party at Dayton's store in Minneapolis in December of 1955. Mr. Brings wanted me to write a version for young people. I had had enough of it, so I did not take on the project.

After I was on Channel 2 for a semester on Christian Ethics, Bill Gentz, then employed by Augsburg Press, urged me to revise the lectures for publication. So, in 1973, when I went to the Institute for Ecumenical and Cultural Research for a sabbatical, I thought I would finally have the time. I tried. I prepared a detailed outline for a book on "Ethics and the Future," in which I would have drawn on my many years of experience teaching ethics. I could not do it. That book was never written. Each time did not seem the right time. I was involved in teaching and preaching and organizational work and knew that I did not have the energy or time.

I continued to write material for my courses in religion and in ethics, for students' use. And in the 1970s my journals became a major writing project, now amounting to almost 280 volumes.

In 1983-84, in connection with my responsibilities as program chair of the 1983 Nobel Conference on "Manipulating Life," I edited and wrote the introduction for the collection of essays by the participants. This fit with my role and came the year I retired from full-time teaching.

I could not take on a writing project during Ruth's final illness and death (1987-90), but after her death I decided to gather and publish, for family and friends, a collection of her writings. It was published by Primarius Limited Publishing with the title, *Morning and Evening* (1993).

After editing the book of Ruth's writings, I worked on my journals kept during her final illness and the year after (covering the time from January 1989 to April 1991). There was no question that I had to put it in book form. It was published in 1994 as *Final Time*.

Esbjojo Appears

DJ: Esbj's playful and imaginative nature was given full sway when granddaughters, Rachel and Rebekka, were preschoolers. They liked scary monster stories, especially Peter Seeger's *Abiyoyo*. One of the granddaughters asked Esbj to tell a story about a good monster, not a bad one. Esbj's response was to create "Esbjojo," a little monster who was funny. In story after story, Grandpa Esbj told the girls about Esbjojo's adventures in Humanland.

Esbj also created stories that were a play on the Esbjornson name, "son of a bear god." This gave rise to another character called Esbjorob who was a messenger from the Bjorn clan that lived way up north. Esbjorob escorted Esbj to the Cave of the Bjorns. These creative "grandpa" stories spoke of the sacredness of life, of reverence and of reverie.

He also loved to tell the girls stories about Robbie and Robbie's World which was the world of Bob's childhood near Lake Superior. These stories had a goal of helping the girls identify with real-life struggles and dreams.

Son of a Bear God

DJ: Esbj adopted the bear as his logo, a symbol of the ancientness of life and the relatedness of all creatures. Esbj collected bears and named his own desk top publishing company, Bruin Press. The pseudonym he wrote under (playfully) was Beargodson and also Reuvin Bruin.

Why I Write

RE: I regard writing as a calling. Writing is what I have done all my adult life. I write even if no one would ever read what I write.

I write for pleasure, yes, making ideas into words and words into stories, poems, and meditations. There is another reason. When I write [in my journals] day by day I deposit a record of who I was in the past. Otherwise I would not remember who I have been. When I look back in my journals and essays at what I have written I have a record of both continuity and change. On the one hand, what I do and think now seems a repeat of what I thought and did ten, 20 years ago. On the other hand, I see developments over the years, sometimes improvements, but not always. Writing gives me a sense of identity.

Finally, I write as a way of meditation. Jon Kabat Zinn says that meditation is repetitive inner work, a tempering force. Carl Jung calls it "soul work," the development of depth of character through knowing something of the tortuous labyrinthine depths and expanses of our own minds.....keeps us on track even in the darkest moments. Years ago I called this exploring "soul space." It seems clear that humans write because we think. "I think, therefore, I am," wrote Descartes. In my case it becomes, "I write, therefore I know that I exist."

My Resources

RE: My life is like a field in which there is buried treasure, which may not be as rich as other fields, but comparisons are irrelevant, because this field contains the particular experiences, and memories that are the raw material of my life to be converted by hard and persistent labor into stories. These stories become wealth which I can give to others, in particular to my family.

Letters

RE: I'd rather write letters than essays. That thought came to me one day when I realized how many letters I had written since I got a word processor. I like letters. They are more personal, more direct and less formal. When I write a letter I am addressing someone I know. Letter-writing is a disappearing art. People use the phone, not the pen. It is hard to develop one's thoughts over the phone. Families have no written record of people they cherish if they have no letters. Letters make up a valuable treasury, because they preserve a story which would otherwise be lost. Will email bring back personal letters? Maybe, but they are usually used to convey terse information, not to elaborate thoughts and stories.

Ruth and I have saved hundreds of letters. These letters tell about activities and express thoughts and feelings that reveal the sort of person as she or he was in the past. Personal letters seem unimportant at the time they were written and read, but years later they are very interesting.

Our family collection contains our letters to each other in the 1940s before we were married, letters from Ruth to her parents and her parents to her during her college years, letters between her parents before they were married, letters from her and my friends and many others. They are precious because they bring to life again those events and persons who have shaped our lives.

There is another reason for keeping letter-writing a live art. The power of the pen is one of the most effective forms of personal power in the history of humankind, and thousands of young people are not learning to use it. If young people are not learning to write, they are losing the power of the pen, which may very well be more powerful than the guns youth are carrying these days. The pen is a means we have to shape our story and world. Writing leaves a record of one's developing story and identity.

Esbj and Edge House

DJ: When Esbj retired, he remained productive. He presented adult forums in congregations and was a speaker at conferences and retreats. In 1993, the Gustavus Adolphus College Association of Congregations (GACAC) established a facility for congregations to use as a retreat center. At that time, I invited Esbj to be a volunteer director of retreats in the "Church House." Esbj did in fact lead several retreats. He nicknamed the facility "Edge House" and wrote a newsletter, "Letters from the Edge," about the purposes of the house.

RE: I call the GACAC Retreat Center *"Edge House"* for several reasons. Its location is on the northern edge of the campus--close enough to other facilities of the College to be available when needed for retreat activities but not in the busy places of action.

Its social location is "on the edge" of the arena of action and the centers of power where decisions are made, away from family, workplace, neighborhood, congregation or wherever there are demanding roles. Edge House lies between college and community. It is one of the outposts of our scattered supporting congregations in the Gustavus Adolphus College Association of Congregations, yet it is connected with the network of persons who are active in many ways and places. It is a place where one can shed the symbols of status and the social supports that prop one up and touch something deeper and quieter, voices within that are drowned by the constant din of dominant concerns.

In a psychological way, Edge House provides persons with a place to put some distance between themselves and the constant pressures of life in the fast lane. Although it is not in some desert or mountain wilderness, it is a quiet place, where we are free from agenda and lists of things to do, meetings to attend. It is a "Sabbath" place providing a break from the action and alternatives to television entertainment. It is a place where one is free to think, to pray, to restore the soul's vitality so drained by constant activity. It is a soul place, too, where the still, small voices of God can be heard in the silence, a place for gathering wisdom of the heart.   *Letters From the Edge*, Series 2, Letter 3

I call the events at Edge House *Gatherings* rather than retreats. *Gathering* evokes scenes of people bringing to one place and time a harvest of wisdom and strength and combining them to create a resource greater than the total of what they brought. It reminds me of the story of the boy who brought his loaves and fish to Jesus, and that gift was multiplied into more than enough to feed a multitude.

Gatherings bring people together who have common interests but with different perspectives. By sharing they add to each other's wisdom and strength. I will tell you why I think such occasions are not luxuries but necessities. It is normal and easy to become controlled by the dominant thought patterns and behaviors of the group in which we function. If we never get away from those patterns we tend to regard them as the way the world is. We occasionally need a point outside our own systems, where we can get a different perspective. In the experience of a gathering we meet, not only at the edge of a common concern, but we also pass over into another person's world and ways of thinking and acting to gain a better understanding of them; and then we come back to our own worlds with fresh understanding of ourselves as well.

Our gatherings are not self-sufficient, for they are subject to an authority greater than any point of view that develops in conversations. The higher authority is the Word. The Word of tradition and the creating Word that seems to come from beyond. A lifetime is not enough to attain wisdom, so the Book of Job reminds us:

Look for a moment at ancient wisdom, consider the truths our ancestors learned.
Our life is short, we know nothing at all. We pass like shadows across the earth.
But let ancient wise people teach you; listen to what they have to say. Job 8:8-9, *Good News Bible*
Letters From the Edge, Series 1, Letter 4

Esbj, 1993.

Chapter Eight:

Final Times

On Healing

DJ:Esbj also called into question common understandings (or mis-understandings) of what it is to find healing in the midst of illness.

RE: I wonder if we do not need to question the aim of curing and distinguish it from healing. What does it mean to be healed? Could it mean acceptance of ourselves as finite humans? Acceptance of our dependence on other humans and also other organisms? Could it mean being freed from the chilling fear of death, rather than from death? Could it not mean being set free to be ourselves, not some paragon of virtue and health and control?

Are we not depriving ourselves of the joy of life by an unreadiness to accept who we are, where we live, and the times in which we live? Is it possible that we need deliverance from our lust for absolutes?--absolute health, absolute knowledge, absolute control? Is it not better to be the servant of the living God rather than the slave of sin? Is this house where we gather to increase our power by drawing on God? Or is it a house of healing? A sanctuary where right relationships are renewed and sustained? 1985

On Medical Ethics and an Approach to Death

DJ: Esbj wrote extensively about medical ethics in his papers and especially in his journals. After laying out several factors to consider in making decisions about the end of one's life or participating in the ending of a loved one's life, Esbj makes the following observations:

RE: Daniel Maguire reminds us that "the question of alternatives is the most neglected of questions. It is the role of man's creative imagination to sense and seize upon alternatives and thus expand the possibilities of life. Imagination is the transcending, expansive faculty of man, his highest faculty, I judge." (*Death by Choice*, 1974, p. 102)

Imaging alternatives for plans, policies and programs is a process that leads to the application of the ethical process to situations. It is the awareness that we are not yet what we could become that stirs a restlessness in us and prompts us to seek new applications. In the process of considering options we are drawn into what may be the most complicated task in the ethical discipline. There are so many factors to consider. A holistic perspective opens up a wide range of possibilities. Consideration of alternatives requires three kinds of assessments:

One, forecasting what may develop, not only as a consequence of the alternative proposals we make but of other developments that might affect them. Concern for consequences prompts the attempt, however difficult, to look ahead to what may happen!

Two, hoping for what we believe are desirable outcomes in the future. Imaging goals that are not yet attainable but are consistent with vision rooted firmly in fundamental beliefs about human destiny is a most challenging task of ethics.

Three, planning programs that are feasible requires making judgments about technical, economic and political problems that might hinder the attainment of goals.

Medical protocols in research and therapy are based on these processes. The options are assessed by weighing them in the balance with the principles that we respect, the analysis of the problem we have made and the feeling of inescapable choice that we experience.

When a decision is made and the action begins, the "luxury" of entertaining various options vanishes. We must live until we die with an odd and disconcerting paradox: we seek an inclusive vision to guide our judgments, but when we decide to act we make exclusions. To live is to choose, and to choose is to exclude. And in that dilemma we may experience the incongruity of human life that makes us either laugh or cry. There seems no way to be entirely in the right--or in the wrong. Human life seems at times a tragic tale, at times, a comedy of errors that somehow turns out right.

However inclusive and extensive are the processes of thought and action, at the center of it stands the vulnerable, limited, animated human person. Each of us stands alone at the moment of decision, yet each of us is accountable to the others in his or her life. Is it any wonder that we devise clever stratagems of evasion, or try to construct foolproof systems to regulate and give warrant to action?

We need to listen to a word of caution from Annie Dillard: "We are most deeply asleep at the switch when we fancy we control any switches at all..." (*Holy the Firm*, 1984, p. 62). We may bristle at this unequivocal statement of our limits, but we must ruefully acknowledge that even our most complete and strenuous efforts to try to direct actions by rules, guidelines and plans are going to fall short. Morality, however completely spelled out, cannot form goodness. Goodness is a gift, a grace, and we see it as an afterthought, if at all. Ethics, even when it is inclusive and deliberately anticipatory, cannot control the future, which always surprises us."

Again Esbjornson quotes Dillard:

There has never been a generation of whole men and women who have lived well for even one day. Yet some have imagined well, with honesty and art, the detail of such a life, and have described it with such grace, that we mistake vision for history, dream for description and fancy that life has devolved. So, you learn this studying any history at all, especially the lives of artists and visionaries; you learn it from Emerson, who noticed that the meanness of our days is itself worth our thought; and you learn it, fitfully in your pew, in church. (Holy the Firm, p. 56).

Yes, Annie, *Yes.* There we hear, in that faithful, hopeful, loving community the story of God that sustains us from birth until our dying day. There we see, if we have the eyes to see, the glory of the Lord, there we see all things whole. There we hear the healing and liberating Word. There we receive the gifts of the Spirit who gives life. There we stand in the presence of the Son of God, Jesus Christ. In him it is always *Yes.* For all the promises of God find their *Yes* in him. (2 Corinthians 1:19,20). June 1, 1982.

Bob's beloved Ruth died in 1990. He who wrote about ethical decisions in facing death, came face to face with those decisions in his involvement in Ruth's illness and dying. In the preface to *"Final Time, A Husband's Reflections on His Wife's Terminal Illness,* Bob wrote:

RE: I invite you into an intimate time of my life as revealed in the pages of a personal journal I kept during and after my wife Ruth's terminal illness and death. It was a time of loss of someone dear to me, a time in which I had to face our mortal and moral limits and to work my way beyond the experience itself to the meaning of the experience.

This account includes excerpts from the journal I wrote as the story was taking place and ethical reflections written during the second year after Ruth's death. The journal is a combination of narrative and meditation which I wrote day by day as I experienced the events. Beginning when my wife Ruth discovered she had breast cancer, the journal covers her final illness until her death in April 1990 and continues with written excerpts after her death, when I was dealing with loss. It describes not only the external story of my wife's final days but also the inner story of my thoughts, feelings and prayers.

The experience of Ruth's illness and death confronted me with not only our mortal limits but with moral challenges as well. Since her death I have been composing my reflections about the experience, not as a participant but as an ethicist trying to make some sense of the moral meaning of what happened. Facing terminal illness and death is not just an encounter with mortality but with moral experience, because it is a time when we cannot escape making decisions about matters of significance to ourselves and others under conditions of uncertainty about motive and consequences.

I have written the reflections as an ethical analysis of significant factors that influenced the decisions and actions that took place in Ruth's and my story. During my years of teaching ethics I saw that the heart of the story is not the recent development of medical technologies that have stirred so much interest in bioethics. Rather, it is the relationship between those who give medical care and those who receive it, a relationship that is a moral affair, not just a medical matter.

The reflections have become an effort toward formulating an ethics for patients, for those of us who enter the world of medical professionals when we need their expert knowledge and skills. When we enter that world, we do not cease being moral persons with rights or responsibility, but we do become engaged in a collaborative effort with the professionals to attain results of importance both to ourselves and them.

These are readings of the heart, by the heart and for the heart. The heart is the core of the self, and the heart is the center from which flows the creative energies of a person's life. I write for your heart from my heart.

What story do I believe shapes my life or, more to the point, *whose* story? It is obvious that I do not live in an isolated story. Mine is but a small part of a larger story, one that began before I was born and continues after I die. How is my story connected with the larger story? Is that larger story my family story, or is it my nation's? Is it even more inclusive, all humanity's or the story of developing life within the cosmic story?

We who at times need medical care in order to live and continue our stories have a very significant decision to make. We must decide that life is "full of sound and fury signifying nothing," or that it has purposes larger than our most colorful and hopeful visions.

From the concluding paragraphs of *Final Time*

Am I better prepared to live in the face of my own oncoming death? I do not know. I haven't been there yet. I cannot foresee future consequences, so I can only say I hope that I will be able to do so with some degree of courage and wisdom. I honestly do not know how well I will respond to the discovery that I am going to die. I have learned something, though.

I had better be well prepared ahead of time because in that final time I may not be capable of clear thought, deep faith or any other human resourcefulness. I may have lost my mind, or be in intense pain that dominates me, or not have enough time to come to terms with my fate. Ruth was surely prepared by her strong Christian faith and experience to face death, but she lost much of her ability and strength to respond during her last days.

If I am aware of dying when my final days come, I hope that the habits of maintaining a prayer life will continue. Even now I often discover myself reciting phrases from prayers, liturgies and psalms without thinking about them. They are like the pulse beat of my heart, almost as familiar and regular. As long as I am able I intend to maintain these disciplines, to live the praying life.

To the extent that I am able, I hope to enter that final time with some sense of my responsibility as a patient. I am convinced that patients have not only rights but duties, including the duty to communicate, even be assertive about one's needs.

Finally, let go, let go, let go. I am trying to learn this ancient art of detachment by ways of meditating that help me to transcend my ties to time and place, to the things I have loved so much. Trust is essential, trust in God's eternal love, and so is faith that in that love I live and move and have my being. Hope is an essential virtue as well, for it is a perspective that enables me to transcend the limits of earthly experience, to imagine far more possibilities than the actualities I have experienced. And finally, love. Love endures. Love is virtually synonymous with life. If I love and when I love, I pass from death to life.

All Soul's Sermon, 1990

Today, in thousands of Roman Catholic churches people are offering prayers for the dead. What's the point? The dead are dead, gone, beyond our prayers--is that not so?

Ashes to ashes, dust to dust. It is obvious that this does not satisfy or silence the prayers, in spite of what people learn in physics, chemistry and biology, the prayers go on.

Why?

We seem to have an irrepressible longing for connections that are broken by deaths. We travel with the dying into the dark valley of the shadow of death as far as we can go, but then they go around a corner and pass from our view, and we cannot follow. Everyone goes alone deep into that valley, and we feel very, very lonely when they go.

We seem to have a strong sense in us that they are valuable. Too valuable to be dumped into a landfill. Too valuable to be forgotten. Too valuable to be annihilated. This sense is the raw datum about us as humans, as empirical a fact about us as our heartbeat.

Ancients taught that humans are souls, fated to be immortal. 'I don't care what they say with their mouths," said the stage manager in *Our Town*, "everybody knows that something is eternal. And it ain't houses and it ain't names, and it ain't heart and it ain't even the stars, everybody knows in their bones that something is eternal, and that something has to do with human beings."

So we dream of reunion with those we loved and lost. We create glorious visions out of our imagination inspired by hope. Or gruesome visions inspired by terror and fear. And most of all we remember. We remember those we love.

An Ethicist and His Health Care Directive

DJ: Ever the thoughtful ethicist, Esbj has written a health-care directive that gives insights into his thinking and values. These directives are shared to help each of us think through our final times.

Hopes for the End of My Life

RE: My understanding of the end of life has been shaped by my experience of being 'The Person' at the side of my wife Ruth during her terminal illness in 1990, when we had to make difficult decisions about her treatment.

My Understanding of the End of Life

I share the fate of all humans, and other forms of life. We are mortal beings who have only limited control over what happens to our lives, particularly over how and when we shall die. We are also moral selves whose fate throughout our lives is to make decisions significant to ourselves and others and the natural and human environments in which we live. This is no less true during our final days. *End* is not only a word for the termination of life but also for the purpose of life. I have no choice but to make decisions about both. Even if I make no decision, I have *chosen* not to do so.

Terminal Conditions

The time will come when my end is near. I will be in a terminal condition when the physician treating me and another health-care professional agree that:

One: I am likely to die within a short time, and life-support treatment would only delay the moment of my death.

Two: I am in a coma from which I am not expected to recover; I have brain damage, and life-support treatment would only delay the moment of my death

Three: I have permanent and severe brain damage and am not expected to recover, even though I can open my eyes, I cannot speak.

Treatments I hope to have and those I do not want when I'm in a terminal condition I want

One: Enough medicine to relieve my pain, even if I will be drowsy or sleep more than I would otherwise.

Two: No action by my doctors or nurses caring for me with the intention of taking my life.

Three: To be given foods and fluids by mouth and to be kept warm and clean.

I do <u>not</u> want

Any of the following life support medical treatments, which may be costly and would only delay my death.

Medical devices put in me to help me breathe
Food and water supplied by medical device (tube feeding)
Cardiopulminary resuscitation (CPR)
Major surgery
Blood transfusions, dialysis, antibiotics, or anything else to
    keep me alive

Treatment I hope to have when I can make decisions but am no longer able to care for myself.

At the end of my life, I may not be in any of the terminal conditions stated above. I may be conscious and able to communicate but not be able to take care of myself. I could live for months in this condition. I would need appropriate care during such a time.

Compassion

"Jesus was moved with compassion." Those who take him seriously also are moved with compassion. I hope they are moved with compassion for me in my distress. Though able to make decisions, I may be vulnerable to coercive forces outside myself, which may not be respectful of my concerns. Or I may be dominated by compulsive feelings of anger, fear, guilt or panic, or show signs of hallucinating. If so, I would like those caring to realize that I do not regard myself to be of sound mind if coercive and compulsive influences are affecting me. I am also motivated by convictions, which are formed from traditions and experience. I hope that those caring for me will honor my convictions as stated in this document, when I believe I am still in sound mind. I, too, am moved with compassion for caregivers, so I hope to make a difficult time easier for those who will care for me when I can no longer care for myself by stating so clearly as I can what I believe about the care I would receive.

Two convictions are the foundation of my statement

Quality. I hope for what I believe is quality treatment, but it may be difficult or impossible in some circumstances to give me all that I hope for, so I don't want this statement to be a statement or demand of my rights. I prefer the words, "wishes and hopes" rather than "want or desire, or demand.

Justice. If the treatments result in excessive financial and emotional costs to family and society, I do not want them. It is not just, not fair, to demand everything for oneself without regard for the effects on others, especially true at my age, for I have had a long and interesting life.

I hope for treatment that is appropriate for four aspects of my being: physical, social, mental and spiritual. The physical has been addressed.

115

My Social Being

As a social being living in a community of persons, I hope for the company of people, especially family and friends. Illness isolates people, and they suffer the pain of loneliness, especially at night. The need to have someone hold my hand or hug me is apparent and to have someone with me when death draws near. I hope also for peace and reconciliation, because final time is difficult and often a time for painful conflicts and unresolved issues in the family. I want to forgive those who have hurt me and to be forgiven by those I may have wronged.

My Mental Being

As a thinking being I have lived in a world of ideas and images. Most persons have such a world of meanings. Because I have been a teacher for many years, I highly value information and insight. I have not only gathered them, I ponder what they mean to me. I value religious traditions, especially the Bible, the arts and sciences; the sources of knowledge and wisdom coming from many streams.

There is a degree of mental distress all through life, but it is more so at the end of life. I may struggle to understand the meaning and purpose of life. There is something irrational about pain and illness, for these ills do not correlate with what I believe to be good and true, or with how good or smart I am. Even medical care is puzzling. All the equipment of the technical medicine model is so marvelous from one perspective and so malicious from another. The emotional and financial cost of effort to keep me alive may actually decrease the quality of my life and work against the inevitable drift into death and dying. I may want to die, deep inside of me, and I need permission to do so.

Sometimes having people around is actually painful, when I may need solitude and silence. I remember scenes where several people were around the bed of one who was sick conversing about matters that were no longer of interest to the sick or dying person.

I hope for friends who are aware that the end of life is a time when a person is beginning to withdraw and needs freedom from social concerns and time alone for time to deal with personal matters.

I hope for the help of a sage or two, who understand that the loss of social usefulness does not mean that a person's life has no meaning beyond that, and who listen to and recognize the mental struggle I may have to understand the meaning of suffering and death. Who he or she would be may come as a surprise--maybe a family member or friend, or perhaps someone young or not a close friend or even someone in the medical world who stops to see how I am doing.

My spiritual self

I also live in a spiritual world, a holy world, where I am related in various degrees of intensity to something or someone that is Holy, beyond all the gods, a splendid and strong presence, arousing both fear and fascination at the same time and inspiring me with the desire to give unconditional trust and loyalty to the Holy One. The One who inspires in me this response is the Lord of life, light and love, Jesus Christ, is the One God's YES to all humankind, and that includes me.

I hope for the soul care from pastors and friends, care that includes
The ritual of confession and absolution.
The holy communion, the feast of thanksgiving, the Eucharist.
Familiar prayers from the Hymnal and the Psalms
The solace of music.
Visual symbols that are windows into the sacred sphere that is in and beyond the senses.

I hope for peace within and around me, a sense of something greater than this life, a gift from God.

After Death Matters

Disposal of my body. I have made arrangement with Mayo Clinic to donate my body for medical research.

DJ: Esbj also included guidelines for a memorial service at First Lutheran and a final burial of remains in Resurrection Cemetery, next to his beloved Ruth.

Carl Daniel, Ruth, Louise and Robert, circa 1956.

Chapter Nine

Esbj as Lover

DJ: Esbj was a romantic who celebrated love in all its forms: eros (desire), philia (friendship) and agape (the pure and unwarranted love of God for humans). In three poems, Esbj celebrates human love.

RE: To Ruth --A valentine, 1973
A promise, prayer and poem
For one within my home, or--
To be more precise--
For one who is so very nice
Who is my home
Where I find rest
Of love and grace
Gleaming in her face.
You are God's gift to me.
It's good to have a place where I am free
To be what I am to you,
Amid the fast pace on the many tracks
Along which we race,
Amid the sounds and sights
The duties and the delights
Of living in this place.
What can I promise but a prayer that I might be,
Not just a poem but a harmony
That gives you shivers of delight
(and not just in bed at night);
A prayer that we can be
What our God finds right,
A true and lovely melody
That hints of glory yet to be.

The Best Wine Comes Late
For Violet and Eric Gustavson's sixtieth wedding anniversary
September 4, 1994
How is it that old bodies, wearing out,

119

Can house such beautiful souls?
Does arthritis deflect affection,
Or a weakened heart diminish adoration?
Not so, not so,
For these aged bottles of good wine!
Are we not, after all, meant to be
Transparent, like bottles, revealing
Eternity, that Love that has no end?
How is it that the best wine
Comes last in the feast of life,
Feisty, deep red and golden white.
Wine is food, the gourmet chef declares,
And so I say to you, dear, long-loved friends,
Who have for so many years
Fed my heart with your love
And shown me how to live
Ten years ahead, before my time has come,
And who show me the way to go home.
God blesses us through you--good, old wine bottles!

Late Love
This poem was written in 1996, six years after Ruth's death.

I have had enough of being alone
I am ready now for the cost of loving,
So little compared with the gain of intimacy,
Of being together with another,
Embraced and embracing.
I know enough by now of the celibacy of love--
Of loving without possessing--
Wherein one is freed by grace
To share and spend wise care with and for
You.
I look and I receive the love light in your eyes,
The surprise of joy a gift I could not demand
And would not want it if I got it.
Love, at this late time, is to enjoy
The sharing of meal and bed,
The rhythm of speech and silence
As we walk and ride,
Fingers touching, side by side,
Laughing, sometimes sobbing.

Will I ever love you well enough to know you?
Know you well enough to love you well?
There is more of you than I can enclose
In my mind and heart.
You are the Other.
Only God can know you well enough
To love you as you need.
I am content to be with you, dear one,
And maybe be for you the love of your life
And live with you the life of love.

DJ: A chapel sermon delivered in 1995 about **"Sexual Intimacy"** contains another poem. The text for this talk had to do with Jesus' teaching about adultery. (Matthew 5:27-28). The last section is reprinted here. He sets up this section by reflecting on the many stories of Jesus and the way he related to women.

RE: It seems that Jesus' respect for women knew no boundaries!

Reflecting on these stories, leads me to share some positive thoughts about sexual relations. Three clues that may help you distinguish between lust for and love of a woman: delight, intimacy and tenderness.

Delight is different from the desire to possess. Delight is love of something good and beautiful. Delight is a form of love that allows the other person to be freely herself. To delight in a woman blesses her, because everyone needs attention, appreciation and affection. To delight in someone or something is different from the desire to possess someone. I remember when I realized this about Ruth, my wife. It was at a New Year's party before we were engaged. We were hardly together all night. I remember so distinctly looking across the crowded room at her and realizing that I was not jealous, realizing that I could enjoy her without possessing her. It was so different from the jealousy that I felt in another earlier relationship whenever my girl was with someone else.

Intimacy is the physical, expressed in genital connection, but it is more than that. It is that precious feeling of special closeness to another person. I remember one of the early dates I had with Ruth before we were engaged. We spent a Sunday together, going to church, then to a restaurant near Lake and Hennepin where we lingered for a long time conversing, and then for a walk around Lake Calhoun as the sun was setting. I don't remember touching Ruth during that day, not holding hands, not kissing her, though I suppose I did. What I remember is that it was a very intimate time together.

Our marriage was one long conversation. Ruth wrote me a letter to be read after she died in which she said how much she would miss our conversations. No wonder I responded so strongly to Thomas Moore's words, "Conversation is the sex act of the soul." We were soul mates, not just sex mates.

Tenderness. Jesus had such a gentle way, especially with women. He always seemed so ready to give tender loving care. It reminds me of a phrase in a love song from my youth. "Try a little tenderness." Tenderness is wanting to avoid hurting that special person; it is wanting to console her when she is hurt, it is wanting to be her best friend when she cannot respond to you.

This feeling of tenderness grew stronger as Ruth and I aged. And never more so than when I was caring for her at home during her last two weeks and on the last night of her life. I once wrote a poem expressing this tenderness.

Daffodils

I would not want to crush
the delicate daffodil
in hands made strong by my delight.
I would not want to rush
with clumsy steps to kill
with indiscreet desire
the sunny smile of April's flower
singing love's rebirth
after winter snows
have covered all the earth.
I would not want to pick
my tall, blithe daffodil.
I would not want her sick
for lack of strength from fertile earth.
I would rather sit still
until I see
the source of her serenity
and power to give so much delight
on a February night.

Ours was a love that grew more supple, subtle and strong, because we were bounded by intimate trust, by a promise of faithfulness, and by a genuine delight in one another in all aspects of our being. I cherish such a marriage for you, a marriage of trust, intimacy and delight, for that is the kind of marriage in which the joy of sex is really the greatest.

On monogamy and sharing love

DJ: In this undated essay, Esbj explores the boundaries for male-female relationships outside of the marriage bond.

RE: It is not a proper interpretation of monogamous marriage to consider it a monopoly on love between the sexes. I am not advocating promiscuous sexual relationships beyond marriages. Indeed, I am accentuating, by stressing diversity, that there is something special going on between husband and wife that cannot be shared by others. There is a unique relationship of intimacy and closeness that cannot be touched by other relationships. But this does not exclude the possibility that both can enjoy and be enjoyed by other men and women, too. No one man, no one woman can be everything to another person. None of us can contain all of the gifts of a generous God that we are able to enjoy."

A Wife's Perspective on "Life with Esbj"

DJ: Ruth Esbjornson was a writer who had a regular column in *The Lutheran* magazine for many years. Here is an excerpt from a column titled, "On Being Conservative" and is revealing about their marriage and Esbj. She begins by telling us what a conservative, careful, reasonable person she is.

I never took a dare in my life--until I got married. Even though marriage was an institution which conservative people had endorsed for many centuries, I thought it might be too radical an adjustment for me--although I was marrying a man of the same national background, same denomination, and same college class!

Since I had always been such a careful, cautious, conservative character, I had had my own way in life--even with my friends. My arguments were always reasonable. I was sure I could manage the same way with a husband.

But I was in for a surprise. He was really unmanageable. Our first argument came when we were going to cut the wedding cake. He had his own idea about how that should be done. My reasonable suggestions did not seem at all reasonable to him. I can't remember how it turned out, but he must have won it because the cake got cut--and I'm sure he didn't give in.

On our honeymoon we were riding along blissfully in the car through the new spring green of the New Hampshire mountains. Somehow we got on the subject of labor and capital (must have been his idea!). We got to arguing so vehemently, he had to stop the car by a grove of pine trees because it wasn't safe to drive. We paced back and forth shouting our points of view at each other. My reasonable arguments didn't impress him in the least. We finally changed the subject and drove off.

This tug-of-war had some violent outbursts early in our married life--my whole way of life was threatened.

Do you remember when the new hymnal came out? It meant a rather drastic change in our church. I thought the old hymnal was fine. I loved the old service. I wanted nothing to do with this hymnal. I practically hit the ceiling (and our church has a high one) when I heard the pastor chant part of the service for the first time. Naturally my husband liked it.

Then he began his usual patient indoctrination with his reluctant wife, and I became an appreciative participant. Worship became meaningful, and my heritage was enriched.

Any music written after Bach was not music to me. My husband, of course, thought jazz was great--in addition to Bach, naturally. Recently we got a stereo record of the liturgy done to a jazz tempo. Had this occurred a few years ago, I would have thought it musically obscene. But because of my conditioning over the years, I found myself putting that record on again and again. When they sang the Nicene Creed, I put it on at full power until it rang across the valley and hit the hills on the other side and my house shook with the glory of it.

I think often about how dull my life would be without a husband who is always excited by new thoughts, new ways of doing things, new people. He is never satisfied to do anything the same old way. He is always sure there is a better way. This means, of course, that he is never contented as I often am with things just the way they are. He is always stretching and always reaching.

DJ: Ruth used this illustration to write about resistance to change in the church. She concludes:

And the church needs to grow. It needs to be challenged in this age of great problems. It needs to be threatened, for that is often the only way it will move at all. To be looking for something new is not deserting the past, it is fulfilling the past--just as Jesus did. The only way to make our ancestors work worthwhile is to be adding to it. The Lutheran, April 8, 1964

DJ: When Esbj wrote *A Christian in Politics* (1955) the dedicatory page read as follows:

Dedicated
To my father, Per Esbjornson,
who showed me what steadfast
devotion is
and
To my wife, Ruth,
who speaks her mind
votes her ticket
and loves with all her heart

A Son's Tribute

DJ: Carl was the second child of Bob and Ruth. He graduated from the University of Iowa and achieved a PhD in literature and poetry. After teaching in several colleges and universities, Carl gave up the academic life for a position of directing Christian education in a church in Bozeman, Montana. He is also a free lance writer who deals with ethical and social issues, especially the environment. He and his wife, Rilla, have two children, Rachel and Rebekka, both graduates of Pacific Lutheran University.

Dear Professor Esbjornson,

I use the title Professor in honor of your retirement and in honor of your superb contributions as a teacher, but you are above all else, my dad and I can most honor you for that because as my dad, you have been also a great teacher. You have taught me openness, tolerance, forgiveness, moral integrity and loving kindness. Not that I always embody these values. The point is these values have come to me through your example. I have been profoundly influenced by them in that, because they are AC-TIVE principles in your life, they have had a dramatic impact on your role as father and your vocation as college professor.

There are, however, two values that you have taught me that I esteem the highest: peace-lovingness and faith. I am very proud of your stand against the arms race and how you have always stood very much opposed to war and military adventurism. That is well and good. Yet, you have taught me something even more essential--the value of being at peace with myself, with friends and neighbors, and with family.

Your success as a teacher is a by-product of your great qualities as a person, the qualities of gentleness, loving-kindness, openness, tolerance and faith. Yes, here is where peace on earth begins. You have shown me a Christian faith that is dynamic and joyful, dynamic in that it is a faith active in love and life and joyful, in that the faith is something to be celebrated, a faith that is redemptive not condemning. The already mentioned values that you have taught me are reinforced by this active faith and through the teachings of Christ which emphasize love and forgiveness. A Son's Tribute by **Carl D. Esbjornson,** *1983.*

Esbj and his daughter, Louise

Louise was born to Bob and Ruth in 1946. In early childhood, she developed diabetes, a condition that worsened over the years. Louise was bright and gifted. She graduated from Gustavus, then worked as a curriculum writer for Augsburg Publishing before going to seminary and becoming ordained. Yet, the combination of diabetes and episodic depression made it a struggle for Louise to do ministry. The result was that Louise's condition was a constant source of anxiety and anguish for many years. Esbj probed the world of mental illness with understanding and compassion. He believed in his daughter's gifts to do ministry and suffered along with her. He prayed for her, hoped for her. Louise died in 2005 from complications of the disease. He grieved her death, but even more so, he grieved that the "bright promise" of Louise was never realized.

Hospitality of the house

"I lived in Valley View dorm and his home was just down the hill from there. He and his wife Ruth, made their home available for so many students. Sometimes it was a haven in the storm." **Janie Hokanson '68.**

"And how can we refrain from mentioning the unusual combination of hospitality, wit and encouragement represented by you and Ruth together. No one who has known you two has any doubt about Gustavus having a heart. No award of the Edgar M. Carlson Award has pleased us more than yours." **Edgar M. Carlson**, congratulatory letter upon the occasion of Esbj's retirement. (1983).

Bob and Ruth's home was open to all, welcoming friends, neighbors and colleagues. Many of us knew the special "porch sit" to which we were invited, featuring ice cream, freshly picked raspberries, iced tea/coffee and delightful conversation. Faculty colleague Ron Christenson coined the term "Esbjerries" to capture the delight of sharing food and conversation with Esbjornsons. Kathryn Christenson wrote this poem which appeared in "Faculty Notes." The phrases in quotes are words Esbj used in chapel talks.

ESBJERRIES
God's berries, occidental
western hedge of St. Peter
summer's berries in July
on the porch with ice cream
God-bearing, even the car
hedges west, berry season over
who but Esbj and Ruth would take
Christ Chapel for vacation on tape
steering a pulpit through Dakota
sermons piercing the Wyoming sky--
"pregnancy is an Advent word"
Mary in December, God-bearing
"who is in the throne room
of your heart if not Christ?"
summer is the advent of harvest
Esbjerries are the crown of July
with which, Ruth, you don't need
a tablecloth, or Esbj, a text
have theology, will travel
have raspberries will root
Faculty Notes 1989/90 No. 4

The Shadow Side of a Good Man
Esbj was, of course, introspective. When he read the draft of this book, he expressed his fear that it made him "too much of a good guy and ignored the

shadow side" of his personality and his teaching." He went on to explain that, whereas he could often hide the shadow side of his personality, his failures as a teacher were more apparent. Not all of his students connected with his teaching style or resonated to his "diggametrip." He was conscious of several "missteps" in teaching. Yet, such consciousness also served to keep him from complacency as he was always looking for new ways to approach a subject. Humility (related to the word humus, or good soil) allows a teacher to avoid arrogance and to be open to correction.

The "Son of a Bear god" in Winter

Janie Hokanson '68, one of Ebj's student assistants, was yet another who re-mained in touch with Esbj for many years, sharing life's journey. Observing him in the "winter of his discontent," Hokanson wrote, "I have been in close contact with him as his health has been failing him and watched how frustrated he has been without a creative outlet for his mind and talents. He has so much burst-ing out of him still, at almost 90."

Still growing

Esbj kept writing and reading while in the Benedictine Living Center in St. Peter. A visit in August of 2007 found him re-reading Bishop John Shelby Spong's, *A New Christianity For A New World.* He was also re-reading a book of former colleague Bill Dean.

These were both writers with whom Esbj had fundamental differences, yet, he read them (and reread them) because he found much merit in each of the books and was willing to consider new ways of looking at matters of faith and life. Unlike others who read some writers only so they can refute them, Esbj reads with appreciation and to see what he can gain in understanding.

The Point of Life

So, Esbj, dear friend, what is the point of your life? What endures? You who have been a mentor to so many, passing the wisdom of the ages on to new gen-erations, is there a summing up point?

RE: Some years ago, shortly after my wife Ruth died, I saw *Shadowlands,* the film about C. S. Lewis' love affair with Joy, who became his wife. In a speech to a woman's group, Lewis talks about the point of life. It is not to pursue happiness, but to learn to love.

This comment helped me to clarify the point of my own life. It is to learn to love well before I die. With that in mind, everything that happens, whether ill or good, becomes material for lessons in love.

I hope that each day I am learning to love better. I have learned at least this much. It takes practice, practice, practice--as much as any art or skill. It is the willingness to keep at it until we get it right, repeating over and over and over again simple exercises in our daily encounters, until loving becomes a habit to one's life.

Letters from the Edge, Series 5, No. 7, 1999

Other Sources

In addition to the papers of Robert Esbjornson and Faculty Notes published by the college, I consulted the following sources:

Anderson, Robert L. "The Awakening Social Consciousness of the Augustana Lutheran Church", *The Heritage of Augustana*, Edited by Hartland Gifford and Arland Hultgren, Kirk House Publishers, 2004.

Erling S. Bernhard, "Augustana's Theological Tradition: Esbjornson, Hasselquist, Olsson, Lindberg, Bergendoff, Carlfeldt, Carlson", *The Augustana Heritage*, edited by Arland Hultgren and Vance L. Eckstrom, 1999.

Esbjornson, Robert, *A Christian in Politics*, T.S. Denison Company, 1955.

Esbjornson, Robert, *Final Time*, Primarius, LTD, 1993

Lund, Donniver, *A Centennial History*, Gustavus Adolphus College, 1963.

Mattson, A.D., *Christian Ethics*, Augustana Book Concern, Revised Edition, 1947.

Jonsen, Albert R., Preface to *The Patient as Person* by Paul Ramsey, Second Edition, 2001.

ABOUT THE AUTHOR

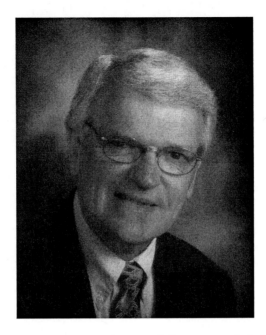

Dennis Johnson is a 1960 graduate of Gustavus Adolphus College. An ordained pastor of the Evangelical Lutheran Church in America, Johnson served parishes in Dallas, Texas, 1965-1977, and First Lutheran Church, Saint Peter, Minnesota, 1977-1985, when he was invited by President John Kendall to join the Gustavus administration. Johnson served as vice president for church relations, 1985-1995; vice president for college relations, 1995-2000; and interim president of the college from 2002-2003. In addition to the B.A., M.Div. and S.T.M. degrees, he was awarded an honorary Doctor of Humane Letters from his alma mater. He and his wife, Carol, live in Minneapolis.

Johnson and Esbjornson have collaborated many times, most especially in developing the programs of the Retreat Center at Gustavus. Through the auspices of Gustavus, a video featuring Esbj on "Living the Praying Life" was created for congregational use. Johnson served as the interviewer. Esbjornson and Johnson also co-taught a January Term course, "Career Exploration in Ministry." Their friendship led to the two working together on this collection.